REVOLUTIONARY RANGERS

Daniel Morgan's Riflemen and Their Role on the Northern Frontier

1778-1783

by
Richard B. LaCrosse, Jr.

with an Introduction by
Harry Kels Swan

HERITAGE BOOKS
2007

HERITAGE BOOKS

AN IMPRINT OF HERITAGE BOOKS, INC.

Books, CDs, and more—Worldwide

For our listing of thousands of titles see our website
at
www.HeritageBooks.com

Published 2007 by
HERITAGE BOOKS, INC.
Publishing Division
100 Railroad Ave. #104
Westminster, Maryland 21157

International Standard Book Number: 978-0-7884-2052-8

To My Parents

for their inspiration and encouragement

Contents

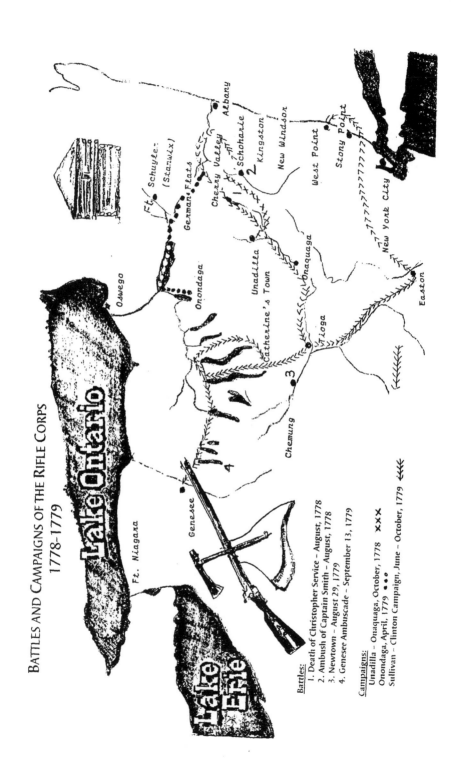

BATTLES AND CAMPAIGNS OF THE RIFLE CORPS
1778-1779

Lake Ontario

Lake Erie

Ft. Niagara

Genesee

Oswego

Onondaga

Ft. Schuyler (Stanwix)

German Flats

Cherry Valley

Albany

Schoharie

Kingston

New Windsor

West Point

Stony Point

New York City

Unadilla

Onaquaga

Catherine's Town

Tioga

Chemung

Easton

1
2
3
4

Battles:
1. Death of Christopher Service – August, 1778
2. Ambush of Captain Smith – August, 1778
3. Newtown – August 29, 1779
4. Genesee Ambuscade – September 13, 1779

Campaigns:
Unadilla – Onaquaga, October, 1778 ✕✕✕
Onondaga, April, 1779 ●●●
Sullivan – Clinton Campaign, June – October, 1779 ⋘⋘⋘

Introduction

From the mid-eighteenth century onward in the Piedmont areas of Pennsylvania, Maryland, Virginia, and the Carolinas, young American men by the thousands matured with the *rifle barreled gun* at their sides as their constant companion and trusted friend. The physical demands of frontier living created men of strength, self-reliance, and independence—elements vital to success when war touched their doorsteps in 1755 and again two decades later.

Most American Revolutionary War historians observe the role of these frontier-bred long riflemen during the siege of Boston and the Battle of Bunker Hill with mixed conclusions. They note the British soldier's respect for and apprehension of the frontiersmen and their *rifle guns*. They also note, however, the unruly actions of these soldiers. Historians often conclude their performance as lackluster during the campaigns in New York and New Jersey in 1776, except, of course, for their singular brilliance in slowing the British advance over Throg's Neck thus allowing Washington and the Continental Army to escape over Kings Bridge. During the *ten crucial days* between December 25, 1776 and January 3, 1777, General Edward Hand's riflemen contributed greatly to American success at the first and second battles of Trenton, as well as at Princeton. No historian denies the key role played by Daniel Morgan's corps of riflemen at the battles of Saratoga the following year. Without Morgan's ability to deliver point fire, the British would not have suffered the abnormal percentage of casualties among their field officers and artillerymen. Morgan could not have effected this damage with musket-armed light infantry alone. He considered both light infantry and riflemen invaluable when fighting as a team. Saratoga proved him correct in his assessment. The riflemen's contributions to the winning of the battles of Saratoga and the resultant open alliance with King Louis XVI of France must not be overlooked. Careful historians also recognize that, in the absence of American artillery, George Rogers Clark's employment of accurate rifle fire accelerated Lieutenant-Governor Hamilton's surrender of the communities in the Northwest Territory during the Revolution.

Author-rifleman Richard LaCrosse, Jr. contributes in this essay a vital but forgotten chapter of our national Revolutionary War history. The role of the riflemen on the American northern frontier from 1778 to 1783, a vital segment in our war for political independence from Great Britain, has not been addressed by national historians. The significance of these farm-bred and trained soldiers, who employed American-made rifles in winning the war along this northern frontier, can now be assessed by students of our Revolution. In this splendid essay, author LaCrosse has contributed a readable and accurate portrait of a little-known and less appreciated segment of the American Revolution.

I conclude this introduction with an obvious, but often overlooked observation on the art and science of warfare. Our army on the land, our navy on the sea, and our airmen in the skies combine to form a war-winning combination in twenty-first-century warfare. So it was with our pioneer fighters in the eighteenth century. Our early marines supported our sailors when attacking enemy vessels. Our rifle units, undoubtedly supplemented our musket-carrying soldiers during our colonial wars to secure our precious freedoms. It must be concluded that the riflemen and the rifle were effective military tools when applied in a specialized fashion. For the special operations of scouting, skirmishing, and sharpshooting, the American long rifleman had no equal throughout the world. Employed in this fashion, colonial American riflemen affected the time it would take for America to fight her way to freedom in the eighteenth century, if not in deciding the ultimate outcome of her conflicts.

Harry Kels Swan
Senior Historic Preservation Specialist
Curator of the Swan Collection of the American Revolution

Acknowledgments

A book of this nature could not be written without the in-depth research of historians, genealogists and researchers who preceded me. Thanks must go to those who collected the primary sources, newspaper accounts, journals and scraps of evidence scattered about that documented the activities of a largely illiterate, or barely so, group of "soldiers"—who, in reality, were backwoodsmen and farmers.

The best primary sources have been the Public Papers of George Clinton for activities in New York State during the Revolution, while the Frederick Haldimand Papers are by far the best view of the war on the northern frontier from the British side. The works of the romantic 19th-century historians like Stone, Sigsby and especially the indefatigable Simms, while requiring a great deal of circumspection, are, nonetheless, indispensable sources of information. One can argue they are in the same category of reliability as military pension accounts, written so many years after the event. However, if these chroniclers had not recorded the vivid memories of old veterans, countless adventures and anecdotes would have been lost forever.

The renewal of interest in the daily lifestyle of the soldier of the time is perhaps best personified by the Brigade of the American Revolution, possibly the finest and most professional organization of living history reenactors today. The author was instrumental in reactivating Captain Jacob Hager's Co., 15th Regiment of Albany County, in

1980, and the memory of that handful of frontier riflemen continues to live on today in the enthusiastic portrayals by these individuals: John and Sue Bardo, Paul Billingslea, Dennis Christiansen, Dan Colondona, James Earley, Dick Essick, Gil Dabkowski, Tom Dabkowski, Jim Ferdue, Ricky Fernandez, Norm Glass, Brian Greb, Ted Kistner, Dwaine Lesson, Tom Ingle, Gary La Violette, Frank Lockwood, Brian and Amy McCoy, Joel Mussman, Sean Otis, Steve Otlowski, Owen Purcell, Bill Redfern, the late Leo Schrader, Judy Schrader and family, Lani Toth, Leigh Ann Toth, Phil Toth, Wayne Thornly, Claudia Troriano, Al Sterling, Greg Tachek, Mike Wager, Bill Wrobleski and David Wrobleski, John Tremain and Patrick Quinn. Perhaps the only criticism that can be directed at the group of men and women is that sometimes they take the field in numbers greater than the actual ten Schoharie riflemen being portrayed! But then there is nothing in the BAR rules about being overstrength. Others who provided help and inspiration include both Ernie and Erv Tschanz, who led our earlier rifle unit, specifically Captain Hendricks' Co., Thompson's Rifle Battalion. Thanks to Stephanie Zembrowski for reviewing the text and providing sound advice, and George Reed for his artwork. And of course, James Morrison, of the 3rd Tryon County Militia, who is virtually a walking encyclopedia when it comes to the Mohawk Valley during the Revolutionary War.

Finally, thanks must go to Jo-elle Jermyn for typing my manuscript and Roxanne Carlson, editor at Heritage Books, who proofread and edited the entire manuscript and offered professional help and advice. Special thanks must go to my good friend and fellow historian, Harry Kels Swan, whose collection of Revolutionary War artifacts and documents is probably the finest such study collection in existence. Finally, thanks go to my wife, Leslie, who arranged and photographed the rifleman's accoutrements that appear on cover, continually tolerates my passion for history, and who, with our daughter Hannah, enjoys reenacting and camping as much as I do.

Part One

The Campaigns and Exploits of the Rifle Corps

1778~1779

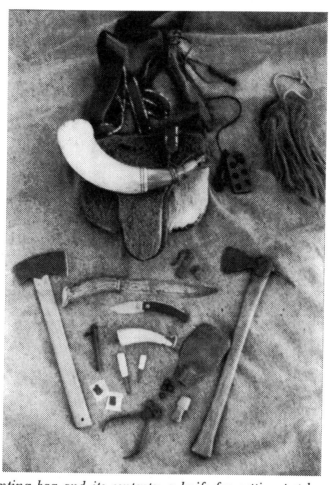

A hunting bag and its contents: a knife for cutting patches, pick and brush set, powder measure and bullet block, powder horn, flint and steel, a folding knife, priming horn, a bullet mould, some balls and the small pouch they are carried in, and some extra flints. On the left can be seen a belt axe, in the center a long knife, and on the right a "spike" tomahawk. Photo by Gilbert Dabkowski.

The Call To Arms

In response to Governor George Clinton's request for Continental soldiers to aid the beleaguered frontiers of upstate New York against the frequent incursions of the Loyalists and Indians, General George Washington dispatched about 300 troops, including two companies of riflemen. These latter, under Captains James Parr and Gabriel Long, constituted about 100 men commanded by Captain Commandant Thomas Posey, the whole under the overall command of Colonel William Butler of the 4th Pennsylvania Regiment.

The remarkable story of this elite corps of riflemen, perhaps overshadowed by the super exploits of a single individual, Timothy Murphy, has never been given due attention. Although Murphy has received his just claim to fame, few indeed, have heard of his fellow riflemen, both enlisted men and officers, who made up this remarkable corps, and who would forge for the regiment as a whole an unparalleled military record.

"Hunting shirts with long breeches...it is a dress justly supposed to carry no small terror to the enemy who think every such person a complete marksman."

George Washington, July, 1776

"The time for which the riflemen enlisted will expire July 1st, and as the loss of such a valuable and brave body of men will be of great injury to the service, I would submit to the consideration of Congress whether it would not be best to adopt some method to induce them to continue. They are indeed a very useful corps; but I need not mention this as their importance is already well know to the Congress."

George Washington, *Letter to the President of Congress,* 1776

"I cannot sufficiently thank your Excellency for sending Col. Morgan's corps to this army; they shall be of the greatest service to it..."

General Horatio Gates
Letter to George Washington, 1777, during the Saratoga campaign

"In this situation Your Excellency would not wish me to part with the corps the army of General Burgoyne are most afraid of."

General Horatio Gates
Letter to George Washington, in Reference to Morgan's Riflemen, 1777

"These [rebel riflemen]...hovered upon the flanks in small detachments, and were very expert in securing themselves, and in shifting the ground...many placed themselves in high trees in the rear of their own line, and there was seldom a minute's interval in any part of our line without officers being taken off by a single shot."

General John Burgoyne, *State of the Expedition,* 1777
[Surrender of Burgoyne at Saratoga, October, 1777]

"Sir, you command the finest regiment in the world."

General John Burgoyne
Words Reputedly Spoken to Colonel Daniel Morgan, 1777.

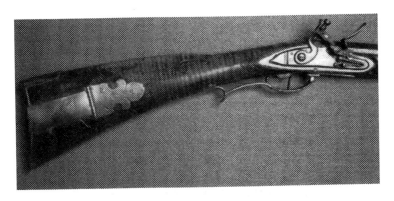

A Revolutionary War period rifle made by John Moll, of Allentown, Pennsylvania. Courtesy of the H. Kels Swan Collection of the American Revolution. Photo by Gilbert Dabkowski.

The Men and Their Weapons

The riflemen were recruited from the frontier districts of Pennsylvania, Maryland and Virginia, and were, in fact, the first official soldiers of the new American army. Although it is sometimes thought they were largely composed of Indian fighting "woods runner" types, most were simply backwoods farmers—young men, usually single, often tall and lean, and ranging in age from their late teens to early thirties. A great many, probably well over half, were practically illiterate, but as a counterbalance, well educated to the requirements and rigors of their lifestyles. The men chosen for officers, on the other hand, were generally older men of stature in their communities and possessed at least the rudiments of an education.

All of these men, officers and men alike, possessed a long, graceful firearm, known later as the "Kentucky," "Pennsylvania" or "American" long rifle, but known at the time simply by the terms "rifle" or "rifle-gun." This arm, then and now has generated a swirl of debate by those who profess to know its merits. The most common firearm of the 18th century was the smoothbore musket rather than the rifle, which could be loaded and fired by a trained soldier four times a minute. As a military weapon it was fitted with a long steel bayonet. Its major disadvantage was its miserable lack of accuracy, an enemy having to be within 50 yards to really risk his life, and even then the odds were probably in his favor. Consequently, it was the bayonet most armies relied upon, although the often-repeated statement that more casualties were inflicted with edged weapons than firepower is highly doubtful.

The American rifle developed by German gunsmiths on the frontier was, on the other hand, accurate to previously unheard of ranges, often to 200 or 300 yards. Requiring less powder and lead for bullets, its grooved, spiral barrel gave it great accuracy. It was not, as some have stated in the past, the "gun that won the Revolution," as only about five to ten percent of the men in the Continental Army were riflemen. It was used mainly by the frontier people of the central colonies, a small minority of the overall population. However, it was not, as some have more recently stated, because of its lack of bayonet and slower loading, an inferior weapon. It was only slower to load when the ball was wrapped in a patch and rammed home, where upon skilled marksman could inflict more damage, though at a slower pace. In a tight situation, however, accuracy was sacrificed for speed by discarding the patch and ramming procedure and simply dropping or spitting the ball down the barrel, enabling the rifleman to load quite as quickly as the musketman. Lack of a bayonet, although a disadvantage, was compensated somewhat by the fact that any rifleman worth his salt could reload and fire on the run. There were very few times, indeed, that Morgan's riflemen, who were the ones later stationed in Schoharie, were caught in a situation where a bayonet was required anyway. The final statement is the rifle's record on the field and

and there the majority of contemporary accounts attest to its superiority in the hands of expert riflemen.

Most of the riflemen, especially early in the war, wore the picturesque fringed hunting shirt of linen, linsey-woolsey, or deerskin, a garment so comfortable and practical that it soon became standard issue for the entire American Army.

Matching trousers or overalls were the most common form of covering the lower extremities, though Indian leggings with breeches or breechclouts were sometimes preferred. Made of a single piece of wool or deerskin, leggings were made by wrapping the material around the leg and lacing them up the outside, often leaving decorative flaps. Generally they came better than half-way up the thigh. Moccasins or shoepacks, but often shoes, were worn by Continental riflemen. The common headgear included low crowned, wide brimmed hats, fur caps, and in windy weather neckerchiefs tied about the head. Military, civilian, Indian clothing and any combination thereof was worn, as reflected in contemporary descriptions and we can see what a motley, ill-supplied, rag-tag, bobtail appearance these men must have made.[1]

Besides their distinctive weaponry and clothing, it was their tactics which truly separated the riflemen from the typical soldiers of the day. Precision ranks of well disciplined troops employed linear tactics which meant they stood shoulder to shoulder loading and firing their muskets as quickly as possible. Taking aim was secondary to speed which, considering the inaccuracy of the smoothbore, made sense. When all else failed, the dreaded bayonet was relied upon.

These rangers, however, had learned their craft through necessity from native Indian warriors. On the frontier, rules of warfare meant nothing, as fighting from cover, laying ambushes and causing massacres was standard. Eventually many of the rifle troops were either broken up or became regular line troops. However, when used in conjunction with regular infantry, riflemen were employed as scouts, light infantry and snipers.

This tradition had its origins in the colonial wars where the rangers under Robert Rogers achieved the greatest fame. However, these riflemen recruited in 1775 not only became the first soldiers of the American army, but the first light troops, or rangers, that continued off and on as needed in the US Army even into the 21st century.

While they may have been revolutionary for being rebels, they were also revolutionary as well for their weapons and their tactics.

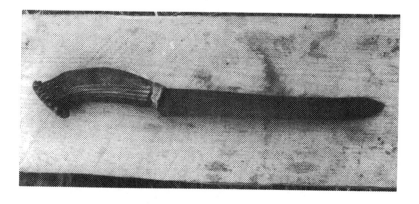

A rifleman's long knife, from the collection of Ted Kistner. Photo by Gil Dabkowski.

Formation and Battle Record of an Elite Regiment

In the winter of 1777, Daniel Morgan of the 11th Virginia was directed by General Washington to raise a corps of Virginia riflemen. Because of Morgan's selection of only the best marksmen as well as apathy of those who had not joined the army, recruiting went slow. However with 180 riflemen, Morgan marched to meet Washington in late March. Stopping at Philadelphia to have his men inoculated against smallpox, he joined Washington at Morristown, New Jersey. To fill the regiment, expert riflemen were chosen from various regiments, most of these being from Pennsylvania and Maryland. These men, on temporary, detached duty, kept their original unit designation, although they often had nothing to do with their original regiments. Under Morgan were his able officers Lt. Col. Richard Butler, Major Jacob Morris, and eight companies with their quotas of officers and men. It has been determined that when enlisted, the total strength in officers and men from Pennsylvania was 193; from Virginia, 163; Maryland, 65; from other states, 87; making a total of 508.[2] Some 50 men and Captain Parr were selected from the "First Regiment" which had originally been Thompson's Rifle Battalion. Some 46 percent were either born in Ireland or of Irish descent.[3] Other major ethnic groups were Scotch-Irish, German, Dutch, and English. Some have stated that some of Morgan's men were armed with muskets, but inquiry into this has failed to find any evidence to support this statement. The confusion possibly arose from the rifle corps often being supplemented with light infantry, or from the actual 11th Virginia, often confused with the rifle corps, a separate regiment under Colonel Christian Febiger, which was a regular line unit. However, the author would appreciate any evidence to support this belief.

Most of the frontiersmen recruited by Daniel Morgan lived in log cabins or houses hewn from the wilderness. The one shown here was originally located near Pine Grove, Pennsylvania, but was moved and restored in upstate New York by the author and his wife. Photo by Leslie La Crosse.

The pros and cons of Riflemen, as viewed by their contemporaries:

"Maryland, December 20, 1775...Rifles, infinitely better than those imported, are daily made in many places in Pennsylvania, and all the gunsmiths everywhere constantly employed. In this country, my lord, the boys, as soon as they can discharge a gun, frequently exercise themselves therewith, some a-fowling and others a-hunting. The great quantities of game, the many kinds and the great privileges of killing, making the Americans the best marksmen in the world, and thousands support their families principally by the same, particularly riflemen on the frontiers, whose objects are deer and turkeys. In marching through woods, one thousand of these riflemen would cut to pieces ten thousand of your best troops."
A Minister of the Church of England to the Earl of Dartmouth, 1775

"It is a certain truth, that the enemy entertain a most fortunate apprehension so infallibly as a frequent ineffectual fire. It is with some concern, therefore, that I am informed that your men have been suffered to fire at a most preposterous distance. Upon this principle I must entreat and insist that you consider it as a standing order, that not a man under your command is to fire at a greater distance than an hundred and fifty yards, at the utmost; in short, that they never fire without almost a moral certainty of hitting their object."
General Charles Lee
Letter to Colonel William Thompson, 1775.

"...about twilight is found the best season for hunting the rebels in the woods, at which time their rifles are of very little use; and they are not found so serviceable in a body as musketry, a rest being requisite at all times, and before they are able to make a second discharge, it frequently happens that they find themselves run through the body by the push of bayonet, as a rifleman is not entitled to any quarter."
Middlesex Journal, 1776

[The] "...shirt-tail men, with their cursed twisted guns, the most fatal widow-and-orphan-makers in the world."
London Newspaper, 1775

"The express, who was sent by the Congress, is returned here from the Eastward, and says he left the Camp last Saturday; that the riflemen picked off ten men in one day, three of whom were Field-officers that were reconnoitering; one of them was killed at the distance of 250 yards, when only half his head was seen."

Pennsylvania Packet, 1775

"Riflemen as riflemen only, are a very feeble foe and not to be trusted alone any distance from camp; and at the outposts they must ever be supported by regulars, or they will constantly be beaten in, and compelled to retire."

Colonel George Hanger
To All Sportsmen and Particularly to Farmers and Gamekeepers, 1814

"The riflemen, however dexterous in the use of their arm, were by no means the most formidable of the rebel troops; their not being armed with bayonets, permitted their opponents to take liberties with them which otherwise would have been highly improper."

Lieutenant Colonel John Simcoe
Simcoe's Military Journal, New York, 1844

"In consequence of the orders of His excellency Gen'l Washington, I now send Major Miller for arms and clothing for the First Pennsylvania Regiment commanded by Colonel Chambers; they never received any uniforms, except hunting shirts, which were worn out and although a body of fine men, yet from being in rags and badly armed, they are viewed with contempt by the other troops, and began to despise themselves. The conduct of the Pennsylvanians the other day, in forcing General Grant to retire with circumstances of shame and disgrace into the very lines of the enemy, has gained them the esteem and confidence of his excellency, who wishes to have our rifles exchanged for good muskets and bayonets, as experience has taught us they are not fit for the field, and a few only will be retained in each regiment which will be placed in the hands of real marksmen."

General Anthony Wayne, *Letter to the Board of War*, 1777

[It is] "...an unfair method of carrying on a war."
William Carter, *British Soldier*, 1775
expressing the typical redcoat opinion
of the use of rifles in warfare.

The new corps soon gained notoriety in the fighting in New Jersey during the spring and summer of 1777. They bloodied the British on the Amwell road near Somerset Courthouse on June 14. On the 21st, the riflemen along with regular troops, drove in a German picket near the outskirts of (New) Brunswick and although outnumbered, dislodged and pursued the enemy to Piscataway, before giving up the chase. Soon after, the British, under General William Howe, withdrew to New York City; Washington fearing that Howe might sail up the Hudson to unite with General John Burgoyne, then pushing up Lake Champlain, sent Morgan's forces to patrol along the Highlands of the Hudson. However, as Howe's next move was uncertain, Morgan's riflemen were ordered first to Philadelphia, and then to Trenton, Germantown, Maidenhead, and back to Trenton again. Washington was increasingly concerned about the northern army under General Horatio Gates and believing Morgan's riflemen to be just the thing to slow down Burgoyne and contest his force of Indians and Canadians, dispatched the riflemen to the aid of Gates. Washington wrote to Morgan, "I know of no Corps so likely to check... (the enemy's) progress in proportion to their number, as the one you command. I have great dependence on you, your officers and men."[4] The corps marched to Peekskill, New York, and there boats carried the riflemen to Albany reaching the American camp towards the end of August.

Their role in the ensuing defeat of Burgoyne and his allies is well known and let it suffice to say that this unit, "a corps of celebrity" and "the elite of the army," as Wilkinson would later write in *Memoirs*, soon became the scourge of the enemy. They chased in the Indian scouts, shot up patrols and pickets, destroyed cattle and horses, and according to some estimates were responsible for inflicting at least half of the casualties (a total of 600) suffered by the British at the Battle of Freeman's Farm on September 19, 1777. In this battle a high proportion of British officers were picked off, and before the end of the day nearly all the artillerymen. When Washington requested the return of his riflemen, Gates replied, "In this situation your Excellency would not wish me to part with the corps the army of General Burgoyne are most afraid of." The riflemen also played a major role during the Battle of Bemis Heights on October 7, in which, once again, enemy officers fell prey to the sharpshooters. It was during this engagement that Timothy Murphy is said to have killed both General Simon Fraser and his aide, Sir Francis Clerke, at a distance of 300 yards. This came at a critical moment during the struggle, for Fraser had been rallying the wavering British lines when a rifle ball mortally wounded him, changing all that, and leading to the American victory that day. It has been stated that after Burgoyne surrendered on October 17, 1777, he warmly grasped Colonel Morgan's hand and said, "Sir, you command the finest regiment in the world."[5]

When the rifle corps rejoined Washington's army at Whitemarsh, Pennsylvania, the regiment had suffered so much from illness, casualties and attrition that only 175 riflemen out of about 500 were fit for duty, many simply not having any footwear to continue. Some served under the Marquis de Lafayette in action near the Delaware River against a German picket, which was driven back over half a mile. Remarking on their enthusiasm, Lafayette exclaimed to Washington that the riflemen were "above even their reputation"[6] running without rest or nourishment in their pursuit.

Although the majority of contemporary accounts attest to the high value placed upon the rifle corps, there are a few exceptions. Many years after the war, British Colonel George Hanger described an action, thought by historians to be the battle of Whitemarsh, when, "Morgan's riflemen came down to Pennsylvania from Canada, flushed with success gained over Burgoyne's army, they marched to attack our light infantry, under Colonel Abercrombie. The moment they appeared before him he ordered his troops to charge them with the bayonet; not one man out of four, had time to fire, and those that did had no time given them to load again; the light infantry not only dispersed them instantly but drove them for miles over the country. They never attacked, or even looked at, our light infantry again, without a regular force to support them."[7] An extensive search has failed to turn up any contemporary account to support this opinion, although it has been accepted at face value by historians as well as those eagerly attempting to debunk the use of the rifle. In fact, Washington himself congratulated Morgan and his men, giving his "warmest thanks" to the "intrepid corps, for their gallant behaviour."[8] One wonders just what battle Hangar was writing about, as nothing else can substantiate his claim that Morgan's riflemen were ever, on any occasion, driven in, as described. At Whitemarsh, Morgan's men fired in the open and then retreated to a patch of woods to reload before repeating the process. Perhaps it was this tactic that gave rise to the story in the first place. Perhaps Hangar, a mediocre officer, was attempting to accomplish with the pen that which had seemed so elusive with the sword. While it may be easy to overly praise the rifle corps, their record more than acquits them of the above behavior.

After the battle near Whitemarsh, the rifle corps, under Morgan "the fox," as one German jaeger called him, engaged in scouting and patrolling activities as the American forces began to move into winter quarters at Valley Forge. After this horrible encampment, in which so few of the riflemen had shoes, a detachment under Captain James Parr earned further laurels in the action at Barren Hill, Pennsylvania, where Lafayette barely extricated himself from a superior British force. When Clinton evacuated Philadelphia in June, 1778, which was seen and reported by the riflemen, Morgan sent in scouts even as the last of the enemy force was leaving. In the pursuit across "the Jerseys," Morgan's men, always in advance, were hot on their trail, picking up some 100 deserters and taking about 30 prisoners. On June 26, the corps attacked the retreating army at Allentown with such force that cannon were quickly called up to repel them. Although active in raiding, scouting and sniping, Morgan's force, through misunderstood and vaguely written orders issued by General Charles Lee missed the indecisive battle of Monmouth on June 28, 1778. After this bloody action the riflemen and light infantry tried to prevent enemy foraging parties from ravaging the countryside along Clinton's line of retreat. On July 1, the rifle corps skirmished briefly with a segment of the enemy rear guard and then withdrew when the redcoat detachment was reinforced.

On July 5, Clinton's army boarded transports at Sandy Hook and sailed for New York City. There is a story, told many years later, but still not substantiated, that a private in Captain Long's Company, David Ellerson (Ellison), later on duty in Schoharie, killed a dragoon, captured a sentry, and took Sir Henry Clinton's private coach while being fired upon by the British fleet off Gravelly Point.[9]

Morgan rejoined Washington's army, crossed the Hudson River at King's Ferry (Stony Point) and encamped at White Plains. For a short time the riflemen were posted in Westchester County opposite enemy-held Manhattan Island. However Morgan was given command of the 7th Virginia Regiment, relinquishing command of the rifle corps. This corps, actually a detached service, was disbanded except for two companies, the men returning to their original units.[10] These two companies, the "remains" of the rifle corps, were captained by James Parr and Gabriel Long, under the overall command of Captain Commandant Thomas Posey. Parr's Company was composed mainly of Pennsylvanians and Long's primarily of Virginians.[11]

Governor George Clinton of New York had been requesting that Washington send Continental troops to help protect the northern frontiers from incessant raiding by British supported Loyalists and Indians. In response, the commander-in-chief detached Posey's riflemen and the 4th Pennsylvania, a line regiment commanded by Lt. Col. William Butler, who was also the supreme commander of both forces.

"Before the return of the Scout I received intelligence
from Genl. Stark of one Smith who had raised a number of Tories and was Marching to Join the Enemy. I immediately detached Capt. Long, of the Rifle Corps with a party to intercept
their March. Capt. Long fell in with them, Kill'd Smith and
Brought in his Scalp, Brought in one Prisoner and it is thought
Wounded a Number. Only one of Capt Long's party was
Wounded. A creek (Schoharie) unluckily being between the
Partys when they Engaged prevented Capt. Long from advancing and gave the rest an Opportunity to escape."

Colonel William Butler, August 13, 1778

The Rifle Corps Arrives in Schoharie

On July 18, 1778, General Washington from his headquarters
at Haverstraw, New York ordered the riflemen and the 4th
Pennsylvania to march to "Wawarsink" in Ulster County,
upon a request from both Governor Clinton and General
John Stark, commander at Albany.[12] They were to
"…cooperate with the Militia and to check the Indians if possible…"[13]

William Butler was the brother of Richard Butler, who
had been second in command of Morgan's Riflemen. They
had three other brothers, all officers in the Continental service. Before the war William and Richard had been active fur
traders at Fort Pitt and the Shawnee town of Chillicothe in
the Ohio Country. Washington placed great confidence in
William Butler. In a letter to General Stark, he wrote that he
would prefer to have Butler in command of the frontier
troops "… as I place a great dependance upon Colo. Butler's
abilities as a Woodsman."[14] Previously, Washington wrote
Congress that "…Colo Butler is an enterprising good Officer,
and well acquainted with the savage mode of warfare; and I
am persuaded whatever comes within the compass of his
force and abilities will be done."[15] Washington also wrote to

Captain Posey that he had drawn a warrant on the paymaster at Albany for $2,500, payable to Posey for his officers and men.[16] The corps paymaster had not applied for their pay.

On July 24th, the rifle corps was at New Windsor, but by the 27th had arrived in Albany. On the 28th, a return of the corps was made and from it we can determine that of a total of 109 rank and file 54 were from Long's Company and 55 from Parr's, 98 of which were present and fit for duty. Of the 4th Pennsylvania total of 131, 128 were present and fit for duty. In the rifle regiment, the following clothing was wanting; 118 shirts, 124 pairs of shoes, 118 overalls, 29 blankets, 30 "napsacks," 60 canteens and 80 hunting shirts.[17] The situation was similar for the Pennsylvania regiment and thus we can see the miserable condition the troops were in. It also sheds light on the type of clothing typically worn. Butler remarked in a letter to Governor Clinton on July 29, that "The Rifle men have hardly a Shoe," and complained that he "...could not be supply'd with a single Article."[18]

Many of the men had their rifles repaired while in Albany and were ready to march by July 30th. Some 50 or 60 troops, evidently riflemen, set off that day, and "...took with them a Brass field P's and an Iron 3 or 4 Pounder..." but there "...is not shot for the latter..."[19] This first detachment arrived in Schoharie on July 31, 1778, Butler and remainder coming in during the next few days. Butler set up headquarters at Fort Defiance, or the Middle Fort, which he believed was the post most likely to be attacked. It had recently been reported by Major Joseph Becker, a militia officer, that Tories and Indians had been skulking about the Schoharie and Cobleskill area. One scout of militiamen which had been out at Harpersfield was pursued, the men scattered, all making their escape.[20]

Lieutenant Colonel Butler intended to carry out Washington's instructions to take the offensive against the enemy and was disturbed when General Stark ordered Colonel Alden, of the 6th Massachusetts, to Cherry Valley, which would make Butler his subordinate. Even General Ten Broeck of the Albany County Militia was willing to serve beneath Butler as requested.[21] As it turned out, Butler and Alden would never form a junction in a campaign and the question of who should command would be unnecessary.

A typical frontier for built of logs and earth, with blockhouses at the angles, and probably not unlike the Middle Fort. Photo by the author.

Upon his arrival, Butler sent out a subaltern and small scout to reconnoiter the new country and to make any discoveries of the enemy. In Jeptha Simms' *Frontiersmen of New York,* it was Timothy Murphy and David Ellerson who apprehended and then shot Christopher Service, a noted Loyalist (or Tory) who lived about 25 miles from Schoharie, near the Charlotte River. Ellerson lived to a ripe old age and related to Simms many of the adventures he and his comrades experienced. Reading Simms closely, we can determine that after Service attempted to resist by swinging an axe at Murphy, which the latter avoided, Murphy at Ellerson's urging to "...shoot the damned rascal,"[22] killed him in the presence of the victim's wife. Simms also believed that this occurred after an ambush on the Schoharie River, but accounts in the *Clinton Papers* indicate the shooting of Service preceded the ambush. It was said at the time that Service was "...a Noted Villain who had Constantly supply'd the Enemy with Necessaries."[23] This scout was also successful in taking four prisoners. Before their return Butler dispatched Captain Long with a party (Simms said about 20 volunteers) to intercept the march of a Captain Charles Smith and a band of Loyalists marching to Service's. According to Simms, Long and his men proceeded cautiously along the east side of the Schoharie and were about 15 or 20 miles distant from the Upper Fort when Smith and his followers were discovered on the opposite bank. Simms wrote that Long, accompanied by Ellerson, advanced quietly and lay behind a fallen log (it would seem questionable Ellerson could have been on both the scout to the Charlotte River and with Long, since the latter was dispatched before the former returned) and waited until the Tory leader, in full Indian costume, stepped into an open piece of ground. "Capt. Long was to fire, and in case he missed his victim, Ellerson was to make a shot,"[24] but Ellerson never got his chance, as "Capt. Long...fired at and shot Smith through the head."[25] The scout quickly advanced and fired upon the Tories and "it is thought Wounded a Number. Only one of Capt. Long's party was Wounded. A creek unluckily being between the parties when they engaged prevented Capt. Long from Advancing & gave the rest an opportunity to escape."[26] However, one prisoner was taken at some point during this operation. Simms said the wounded man was Judge Abeel who received a musket ball in his shoulder. Smith was scalped and Captain Long sent the trophy to General Stark in Albany.

Sketch of the Upper Fort, by George Reed, based on Rufus A. Grider, 1887. This fort was commanded by Captain Jacob Hager and was considered to be the best built of the three forts of the Schoharie Valley. Extra strength was created by the construction of "crib work" which consisted of parallel walls of horizontal logs filled with earth.

Sketch of the Middle Fort, by George Reed. Also known as Fort Defiance, this post became the headquarters of Lt. Col. William Butler in 1778 and was where most of the rifle corps and 4th Pennsylvania was stationed. It successfully withstood a fierce British and Indian attack in 1780 and was the scene of Tim Murphy's near mutiny.

Sketch of the Lower Fort, by George Reed, based on Rufus A. Grider, 1887. A stockade and blockhouses strengthened the stone church (1772) that still exists today and is a museum. Sharpshooters were placed in the steeple during the October 1780 attack.

Among the prisoners taken by the first scout were found some incriminating "letters from Smith to (Walter) Butler and Brant, informing them that he "would meet them at Service's on Sunday following with a Number of Torys who he had engaged. I also had intelligence that the intention of the Enemy was to March in a Body to Service's & there divide one party to Attack Cherry Valley & the other this place." Colonel Butler detached "...Major Church with 120 men to a canoe place about 5 miles beyond Service's (which they must attempt landing at) to lay in Ambuscade & prevent their landing."[27] Perhaps because of their provisions at Service's now cut off and the likelihood of hearing of Smiths' defeat, the enemy forces were persuaded to quit the area. After waiting in vain for the enemy's arrival, the Americans drove off all the cattle in the area considered as supplies for the enemy. Some 52 head of horned cattle and 49 horses were taken. This operation is said to have been the first offensive mounted against the enemy in this quarter of the frontier.

Colonel Butler complained, "Except in these instances I have been Obliged to Act totally on the Defensive; the little dependence that can be put in the few militia that do turn out, the disaffection of most of the Inhabitants to us, the distance and Wilderness of Country that we have to pass thro to the Enemy without the Necessaries for such an expedition, makes it very difficult in my present situation to act otherwise."[28] Butler, however had a plan for an offensive against Onoquaga (or Oquaga) and Unadilla which he would soon put into effect. Since the arrival of the troops, numbers of "disaffected people" came in begging for protection and taking the "oath of Fidelity" to the states. The livestock taken during the latest operation were sold by Butler, who held on to the money until it was decided whether the money should be divided among the troops as a reward or submitted for the public good. It was often the custom for partisan detachments to divide the profits from plunder and this idea was supported by Butler, at least in this case, because of the great effort and fatigue in bringing off the livestock and "the Benefit there derives from rewarding good troops."[29] However, others believed this could encourage the plundering of innocent parties, among these the "Commissioners of Sequestration" in Albany County. Governor Clinton sympathized with both parties, but regardless, the practice continued.

Another problem arose upon the death of a Hermanus Dumon, who, returning from a hunting trip with John Barrow, was captured by a scout of riflemen under Captain Posey near present-day Arkville in Delaware County. On August 26, Colonel Butler had three scouts out consisting of 150 men who patrolled the area near the head of the Susquehanna and Delaware Rivers. Their objective was to suppress activities of Loyalists and destroy Indian settlements. One of these parties under Posey took these prisoners and turned them over to Colonel Harper's militia. In an attempt to escape Dumon was killed and Barrow wounded. It was found however, that this Dumon had been a spy providing intelligence to the authorities of Ulster County and had mistaken the riflemen for Tories, who had thought the same of Dumon, thus the possibility of the Americans killing their own spy was investigated. As it was believed Dumon was also aiding the enemy, the case was dropped and Posey, of whom Governor Clinton wrote, "I entertain too good an Opinion [sic] of him to doubt the Propriety of his Behaviour on that Occasion,"[30] was fully exonerated.[31] The riflemen had, however, been accused of looting the inhabitants, and Posey made them give up several suspected items.[32]

Since the operation against Smith and Service, Colonel Butler had noted that "Every thing is very Quite [sic] here at present."[33] Perhaps the enemy preferred easier targets than those defended by regular troops. The oath of allegiance Butler was giving to the disaffected persons was sent by the

"Minutes of the Commissioners for Detecting and Defeating Conspiracies in the State of New York,"[34] and also provides us with some insights into other events of the time. Some of Butler's men took one Hugh Alexander and Janet (or Jenny) Clement, suspected of being Tories and going off to the Indians. They, along with John Docksteder, were sent to the gaol in Albany to await their trial before the Commissioners of Conspiracies.[35]

It was at about this time that Colonel Butler had spies out to watch the Indian and Tory settlements at Onoquaga and Unadilla. An interesting account of a heroic and brave individual was included in a letter to the Governor. John McKenzie (McKenna), a rifleman of Captain Parr's Company, set out for Unadilla on August 17, arrived there on the 19th and there blended in with the enemy forces. McKenzie must certainly have been aware of his fate if exposed on this dangerous assignment, but he executed it faithfully. He met a number of his acquaintances who had joined the Tories (probably from Pennsylvania), and without arousing suspicion extracted from them that there were 400 to 500 whites at the settlements and although they were not sure of the Indians, some thought 500 or 600, others that there were fewer. McKenzie also learned that Walter Butler was at Chemung with 1100 Indians, and Brant commanded at Oquaga but would not make an attack unless the British made a sally from New York City. On the 24th, this forgotten hero somehow slipped away and on the 29th gave his sworn testimony.[36]

A small scout of 4 men was sent out in September, who returned with three prisoners taken near Unadilla. These prisoners gave intelligence that the enemy force at that place was 300, at Onoquaga about 400, but the forces at Chemung they could not ascertain.[37] Armed with this information, Colonel Butler was several steps closer to putting his plan to destroy these settlements into execution.

Onoquaga and Unadilla

The clothing that Colonel Butler had ordered in August had still not arrived and the threat that it would not arrive before winter was very real. Yet with his men "...Almost bairfooted and Naked,"[38] the American commander was determined to carry out his mission. An expedition under Colonel Thomas Hartley moved up the Susquehanna and entirely destroyed three principal Indian towns—Queen Esther's Town, at the mouth of the Chemung River, nearby Tioga, and the village of Chief Eghobund. Queen Esther's Town and Tioga were considered the southern door of the Iroquois Confederacy and had been the staging areas for raids launched on the Pennsylvania settlements. After beating off a counter-attack, Hartley and his troops returned to Sunbury in Pennsylvania with slight loss. A party of pro-American Oneidas had destroyed an enemy settlement near Unadilla as well.

THE CAPTIVE MOTHER AND BABE.

The campaign against Onoquaga and Unadilla was chronicled in two major accounts, Colonel Butler's and mapmaker Captain William Gray's. It is largely from these that the following is based.

On October 1, 1778, Lt. William Stevens of Captain Parr's Company, was detached with 12 men along with a subaltern and 16 privates of the militia to the outskirts of the valley to guard roads and passages to prevent intelligence from being carried to the enemy.[39]

The next day, 122 men of the 4th Pennsylvania, 56 of the rifle corps, 18 of Lieutenant Dietz's Company of rangers and 7 militiamen, guides and packhorsemen, a total of 203 men, began their march with six days provisions on their backs and five on their packhorses.[40] The roads soon became poor and the weather turned to rain as the men reached the headwaters of the Delaware on the 3rd, and they followed it for two more days before striking across the mountains for the Susquehanna. On October 6, only eight miles from Unadilla, Lieutenant Stevens and Lieutenant Reuben Long, the latter of Captain Long's Company, took out small scouts to make prisoners of some inhabitants a few miles away. These parties later came back with a prisoner and from the latter Colonel Butler learned that the enemy had left several days previous for Onoquaga. The next morning Stevens and a few men left for Unadilla to capture one Glasford, a Tory that could be used for a guide. Again, the men were successful and the Americans went on to Unadilla, wading the Susquehanna three times to get there. On the last crossing, the advance party discovered a fresh footprint, evidently an enemy scout who it was feared could have alerted the foe. Three runners followed the track for eight miles, but came back at nightfall. At about 10 p.m., Lieutenant Stevens, evidently an active and capable rifle officer, was once again ordered out to reconnoiter the country around Onoquaga. Stevens spied upon the settlement from the adjacent mountains and the next day, the 8th, gave Butler a good description. During the early morning hours a heavy rain had soaked the troops and their arms, and the latter had to be dried and cleaned before advancing. Shortly before 11 p.m., the troops crossed the Susquehanna, which at this place was about 250 yards wide and waist high. Butler, who understood the uses of both rifle and musket troops, and fearful of an ambush while crossing, ordered the riflemen to march in front and, if discovered, to file off to the right and left to attack the flanks, while the "musketry with fixed bayonets" charged the center. They crossed over and without interruption took possession of the town. Numerous campfires were built in an effort to dupe the enemy into believing there were more troops, and the men "...fared sumptuously, having poultry and vegetables in great abundance." This village consisted of "...about 40 good houses, square logs, shingles and stone chimney, good floors, glass windows."

The next morning Major Church of the 4th Pennsylvania, and some men crossed over the river and burned "...ten good frame houses, with a quantity of corn, and brought off some cattle." Some of the packhorses had strayed and when, without arms, the owners went in quest of them, one was shot dead by an Indian, and was found "...with part of his brain out." Butler sent captain Parr about 3 miles lower "to burn a castle" (an Indian village) and "to deceive them by a feigned pursuit," as it was feared the enemy was now in the vicinity. After Parr's return, Onoquaga was burned and the crops destroyed. At 3 p.m., the troops recrossed the river, this time with the musketry in advance. All stray dwellings encountered were soon put to the torch.

On October 10, during another incessant downpour with the creeks and rivers rising, there was great difficulty returning. One creek was so high the horses had to swim and trees were felled for the men to cross. In an attempt to cross the Susquehanna, the men had to be mounted on horses. It took 20 trips to get across, with the horses sometimes swimming. It is perhaps noteworthy that seven muskets were lost in the crossing, but no mention is made of rifles meeting the same fate. Part of Unadilla (on the south side of the Susquehanna was burned except for Glasford's and a saw mill and grist mill.) On the 11th, the men rested and cleaned their arms, while a raft was built to transport Lieutenant Long and a private, who, on the next day, crossed over and burned the rest of the settlement. Finding it impossible to cross the Delaware, the troops attempted to cut across the country and became lost. They found their way the next morning and continued the return march, with no provisions. The men parched an ear of corn apiece on the 15th, and on the 16th returned to Fort Defiance (the Middle Fort). As a compliment to his brave troops, Butler ordered 13 rounds of cannon fired, and a "feu de joie" or fire of joy. This expedition of "Near 300 miles," was waged under the most trying of conditions, yet was completely successful. The Tory and Indian force, several hundred strong, had, as it turned out, been raiding farther down the Delaware River, otherwise it might have severely mauled or entirely destroyed the little invading force. With winter approaching, this important place of rendezvous virtually obliterated, the enemy was forced into an uncompromising situation.

For a brief time Colonel Butler believed the frontier in this quarter was safe for the remainder of the year, however the picture soon changed as the friendly Oneidas began to bring word of a retaliatory raid. The settlement at Cherry Valley seemed the likely spot, but Colonel Ichabod Alden who commanded there with some 250 Continental troops refused to take heed. Alden sent Capt. Parr with a letter to Butler in Schoharie stating that he would reinforce him if attacked. Butler detached the rifle corps to the Upper Fort, the likely place for an attack, and sent out six small scouting parties to discover any approach of an enemy force. As it turned it out, it was Alden who was attacked in the surprise assault of November 11. He was killed along with many of his

officers and some of the settlers, followed by massacre of
some of the settlers. Upon word of this outrage a detachment of militia and a company of riflemen were dispatched
to Cherry Valley, but before they arrived the raiding force
had departed. They were too late to do more than collect the
fugitives hidden in the woods and bury the dead.[41] The defenders had not managed to inflict a single casualty on the
enemy. Both Walter Butler, the Tory, and Joseph Brant attempted to excuse the behavior of their troops, their justification being their exasperation at the loss of Unadilla and
Onoquaga, as well as at Chemung. This is an absurd justification as the latter were sound military targets, hardly a reason
for the killing of non-combatants. It was simply a reversal of
what the Tories and Indians had been doing to the frontier
settlers and the enemy had decided they did not like it.

Winter of 1778 - 1779

General Washington had been much pleased that Butler "effectually destroyed the Settlements of Anaquage and Unadilla..."[42] but had realized "...their distressed situation and the approaching cold season make a supply indispensable in an expedition of this nature."[43] However, the expedition had been successful without supplies, making it all the more remarkable. Yet the clothing shortage still plagued the troops, and all hope of receiving them from Albany was lost. On October 17, Washington ordered "80 suits of Uniform, a proportion of shirts and Stockings and 50 blankets and fifty pairs of shoes"[44] for the riflemen, to be drawn from the stores at Springfield. What exactly "suits of Uniform" were is unclear, but possibly included regimental coats. On October 17, Washington feared they were delayed,[45] but on November 20 hoped they arrived.[46] Even as late as January 25, 1779, Washington was unsure if they had received their full share of clothing, stating the deficiencies "...shall be sent up to them."[47]

The Commander-in-Chief had also wanted the rifle corps, the last remnants of Morgan's force, to be dissolved, as had the other six companies the previous summer. In a letter dated December 20 to Major Posey, in which he ordered him to join his regiment, the 7th Virginia, Washington said he had written the commander in Albany expressing his desire to have the corps disbanded if its services could be dispensed with and the men returned to their respective regiments. Washington said it was for the Albany commander to decide, but "I am however anxious it should take place."[48] Washington wanted his men back, but wrote on January 25, 1779, to General Clinton, "Under present circumstances I would not have you send the Rifle Corps down, if they have not received their full Clothing."[49] He counter-ordered their march. It had been suggested to move the rifle corps to the Wyoming Valley of Pennsylvania, but this never came about and the riflemen spent the winter in Schoharie. That Washington may have disliked riflemen cannot be the answer to why he was so eager to see them disbanded. In a letter dated March 3, 1779, he wrote that active rangers who are marksmen are "...infinitely preferable to a superior number of Militia."[50] He merely wanted to swell his number confronting the British in New York City and preferred them to be musketmen, notwithstanding their battle record.

Meanwhile, Parr was promoted to major upon Posey's return to the main army and Lt. Michael Simpson was promoted to captain to replace Parr. Captain Gabriel Long had also been ordered back to his original unit and resigned on May 13, 1779. His place was taken by Captain Lt. Philip Slaughter, though the company was still considered Long's. The confusion arising from these changes in command has resulted in many historians stating there were three or four rifle companies in Schoharie, when there were never more than two.

The winter may have been somewhat more pleasant than the misery experienced in former encampments as the men were quartered in relatively warm barracks, and some may have received new clothing. The winter was mild, and unlike most military posts, there was the attraction riflemen were always known to pursue—women. At least ten riflemen returned to the Valley and enlisted in the local militia, some marrying local girls. One of the first, according to church records, was the marriage of Pvt. Joseph Evans to Maria Becker that winter. Eventually Timothy Murphy married Margaret Feeck; David Ellerson married Sara Begraft, William Leek married another Maria Becker (who, according to Simms had been married to a Tory), John Wilbur married "a Miss Mattice," Philip Hoever married Susannah Vrooman. There were possibly several others whose records were not found.[51]

Times were not always hazardous. Ellerson related a story to Simms that involved soldiers and their officers but does not make clear if it was when he was with the rifle corps or the militia. Among the soldiers at the Middle Fort were two fiddle players. When the officers resolved to have a party, to the exclusion, of course, of the enlisted men, the latter determined to have their own the same evening. Some ten gallons of wine, among other "necessaries," were brought from Albany. Ellerson claimed he spent $30, an immense sum then, on wine, and stated that others may have spent a like amount. The men then "...succeeded in getting the ladies all away from their epauletted superiors, so as entirely to prevent the latter from dancing."[52]

Monthly strength reports also provide us with a glimpse of the rifle corps at this time. At times the corps was lumped together with the returns of the 4th Pennsylvania, leaving us little to determine. However, the former are specifically reported for the months of March, May and June of 1779. In the January return, four men had deserted from the total count of the two regiments. In March, the rifle corps numbered a total of 122 men, with 104 present and fit for duty, 7 sick and present, 1 sick and absent, 9 on command, 1 on furlough, and 3 recruits picked up—a total of 111 well and sick in Schoharie. There were no deaths or desertions. For April, 1 deserter, 1 recruit, and no deaths were listed from the combined regiments. In May, with the arrival of spring the outlook began to change. For that month, out of a total of 120, 107 were present and fit for duty, 9 were sick and present, 1 was sick and absent, 2 were on command and 1 was furlough. Two had deserted, but this was more than balanced by 12 recruits—a total of 128 well and sick in Schoharie. It is a mystery who the new recruits were and one wonders if they were local men who were among the minority of the settlers in the area who possessed rifles or if men with smoothbores were being allowed into the regiment. It is also interesting to note that at least 15 enlisted in the rifle corps and at least 24 others in the 4th Pennsylvania, a total of 39 between the two regiments.[53]

Into the Onondaga Country

As it was believed the Onondaga Indians had been participating in the bloody and outrageous attacks on the frontier inhabitants, or at least aiding and providing a base for the other nations of Indians that were raiding, a punitive expedition was planned under General Washington's orders to lay waste their settlements. The primary sources for this campaign are the journals of Captain Thomas Machin and Lt. Erkuries Beatty, the latter of the 4th Pennsylvania, and Colonel Goose Van Schaik's official report.

On April 6, 1779, a company from the 4th Pennsylvania and a company of riflemen under Lt. Elijah Evans assembled at the Middle Fort and moved out at about 9 a.m. They proceeded to Cobleskill, arriving there at about 4 p.m. At this place they were joined by a company from the 5th New York under Captain Johnson, who had been stationed at the Lower Fort. Johnson took command and the next day the three companies went to Canajoharie. On the following day they moved to Fort Plank where wagons were procured to carry the men's packs. The troops encamped within a few miles of Fort Herkimer, which they reached the next morning. Here they joined several more companies of New York and Massachusetts men, and with Captain Leonard Bleeker of the 3rd New York in command, marched 13 more miles before encamping that night in the woods. The next morning the troops marched 6 miles to the site of old Fort Schuyler (Utica) and then another 16 miles to another Fort Schuyler (or Stanwix, located at present Rome, New York), arriving at about 5 p.m. After being saluted by three pieces of cannon, four companies encamped on the glacis and two were quartered in the fort with all of the officers.[54]

Here they remained encamped for several days. On April 18, the nearby Oneidas were sent on an expedition to attempt the capture of the British post at Oswegatchie on the St. Lawrence River. It had been feared they might give word of the proposed expedition against the Onondagas and were thus sent off. At the same time some 30 bateaux arrived from which the men drew three days' provisions, and were ordered to hold themselves in readiness.[55]

On April 19, about 558 men left Fort Schuyler under Colonel Goose Van Schaik, Lt. Col. Marinus Willett, and Major Robert Cochran. Again the weather refused to cooperate as the troops departed at sunrise in a blizzard. The bateaux, which had been carried over the portage the previous night to Wood Creek, were now sent down that important stream guarded by some soldiers, while the rest of the army followed the creek and then went across country before reaching Oneida Lake, a distance of 22 miles (this was in the vicinity of modern-day Sylvan Beach). A couple of miles before entering the lake, the bateaux, after several hours' waiting, finally caught up, having been obstructed by many fallen trees and branches, whereupon the army embarked at about 10 p.m. A cold head wind greeted the troops as they made slow progress across the lake, averaging about two miles per hour. They reached "Posser's Bay" at 8 a.m. on the 20th and beached their craft at the Onondaga Landing, opposite to old Fort Brewerton at about 3 p.m. After leaving a sufficient guard for the boats, the troops marched in two columns, the "...Rifle Compy. To divide upon each flank." That night they encamped in the cold, dark forest without fires and with "...the strictes orders to keep silence," as they lay upon their arms for fear of surprise. The troops had passed through the vicinity of the present towns of Cicero and Clay and were perhaps nine miles or so south of Fort Brewerton.[56]

The march was resumed early the next morning, April 21, and after making six miles, Captain Graham's Company of light infantry, of the 1st New York, was sent in advance. The American force then continued on to "the Salt Lake," or Onondaga Lake, waded an arm of it 4 feet deep and 200 yards wide and pushed on to Onondaga Creek ("small but deep"), which had to be crossed on a fallen log serving as a bridge. An Indian was taken near here from whom "...we got some Information..." They continued on when word was received that Graham and his men had "...caught one Squaw and killed one and had taken two or three Children and one White man..."[57] However, the alarm was now given and the troops hurried on with all dispatch in an attempt to take as many prisoners from the three towns which largely comprised the Onondaga population.[58] The Indians made but a feeble show of resistance, fighting a brief skirmish "...near Mickle's Furnace on the west side of the hollow. The Onondagas were pursued into the swamp eastward of there, with a trifling loss."[59] The villages were sacked and plundered with some 50 houses burned. Crops were destroyed and livestock slaughtered. Colonel Van Schaik reported of the enemy loss, "Twelve were killed and thirty-four, including one white man, were made prisoners."[60] Among the killed was "...a Negro who was their Dr..."[61] A swivel gun was damaged and "...

about one Hundred guns, some of which ware Rifles, was among the Plunder, the whole of which, after the men had Loaded with as much as they could carry, was Destroyed..."[62] After the destruction of the towns, the troops, laden with plunder, began the return march by retracing their route across Onondaga Creek in the same line of march as before, but with the prisoners in the center and the riflemen in advance. Along the creek they were fired on by about 20 warriors from the other side, "...but the Rifle Men soon Dispersed them killing one of them..."[63] Recrossing the creek in two places, as well as the arm of the lake previously referred to, the army encamped by the side of the lake. The precise spot of this encampment of the 21st is unknown, but may have been near a spring of water a little below Green Point, or at least, some point on the high ground between present Salina and Liverpool (possibly on or near the site of Count Frontenac's fort of the previous century).

The next day the troops made their way back to their bateaux. They reembarked and made their way to "Seven Miles Island," known today as Frenchman's Island, and there encamped.[64]

The next day, in fair weather, they crossed Oneida Lake and land two miles up Wood Creek where two companies guarded the boats up the stream, while the others cut across country, marching seven miles to encamp on Fish Creek. At about noon on April 24, the troops returned to Fort Schuyler where they were saluted by three pieces of cannon. Each company took its old quarters. The Americans completely effected the object of the expedition, that is, the total destruction of the Onondaga towns and the taking of prisoners in less than six days, over a distance of 180 miles without the loss of a man. Militarily, it was a perfectly executed operation, as successful as Butler's destruction of Unadilla and Onoquaga. However, as a strategic enterprise, it is questionable. Although Colonel Van Schaick reported that some of the more intimidated Onondaga warriors had come over to the American side and were being used as scouts against the British, and that American scalps had been found in their villages, justifying to a degree the raid, the Onondaga nation as a whole were now definitely on the side of the British and would seek revenge. However, at the time it was hailed as a great success and so wrote General Washington in his general orders for May 8, 1779, "The good conduct, spirit, secrecy and dispatch with which the enterprise was executed do the highest honor to Colonel Van Schaik and the officers and men under his command and merit the thanks of the Commander-in-Chief."[65]

An Iroquois warrior in accurate 18th-century dress. During the American Revolution the Seneca, Cayuga, Onondaga and Mohawk Nations sided with British and Loyalists, while the Oneida and Tuscarora largely favored the Americans. The Schoharie Indians were a branch of the Mohawks. All told, the Six Nations could muster fewer than 2000 warriors. Photo by the author.

On April 25, the plunder was equally divided between each company. On the 26th, the troops went down the Mohawk River to Fort Herkimer. They stayed at Major Jelles Fonda's on the 27th, and at Schenectady on the 28th. The next day the rifle company and Captain Gray's Company of the 4th Pennsylvania left overland and reached the Middle Fort later that day after a tour of three weeks.[66]

Intermittent Activities

The Onondaga Expedition was but a precursor of what was to come. A plan was being developed in which it was hoped the entire Indian country of central and western New York would be laid waste. Lt Col. Butler had been briefly recalled to headquarters at Camp Middlebrook, New Jersey, but was back in Schoharie by June and promoted to a full colonelcy on June 23, 1779.[67]

With plans for the upcoming expedition into the Indian country, Washington realized the need for the riflemen and gave orders for the corps to remain intact. On May 8, he had written to Major Parr, "As the exigences of the service require, that the Two Rifle companies should continue detached from the Main Army for some short time. I request you will remain with them, till you are farther advised by me."[68]

A return for June of 1779 gives us yet another glimpse of the complexion of the rifle corps. Taken at Canajoharie, after the expedition had begun, we learn that out of a total of 120 officers and men, 78 were present and fit for duty, 6 were sick and present, 1 sick and absent, 1 on furlough and 34 on command or extra service.[69] Among the latter were probably 15 riflemen left at the Middle Fort and perhaps others on scout or detached duty. All those on furlough had been ordered in.

An incident occurred at about this time which can serve as an example of the intrepidity of many of the regiment's men. In the "Minutes of the Commissioners For Detecting and Defeating Conspiracies in the State of New York, the Albany County Sessions," we find a case illustrating their evident belief in "guilty until proven innocent."

One Samuel McFarlan "...being looked upon as a Person of a Suspicious Character was apprehended..." by a Captain McClure in the Albany area. Upon his examination, held on June 8, 1779, McFarlan claimed to have previously belonged to the Continental Army under Captain James Parr, and was regularly discharged. He also said he was captured by the enemy in the spring of 1777 at "Elizabeth Town," New Jersey, but had lately made his escape. He had come to the area to deliver letters from Governor Livingston to General McDougall. A letter was sent to Schoharie to Parr but evidently it did not reach him before he left on the Indian expedition. Meanwhile, McFarlan was tossed into gaol on suspicion of being a spy and/or a deserter. On June 11, McClure testified that he had found on McFarlan's person a silver watch and $450, a large sum in those times.

On July 28, after a month and a half of confinement, the commissioners reported the escape of McFarlan, and soon began to suspect several "disaffected" inhabitants of aiding him in his break out and concealment. The blame for the escape was shifted from one to another as each attempted to point a finger at the other. But as no evidence was found, they were eventually released.

Then, on November 10, 1779, in what must have been a dramatic moment, but is only dryly recorded, McFarlan boldly reappeared before the commissioners and produced "...proper Credentials of his Character which being Satisfactory ordered that he be discharged."[70] How McFarlan obtained these papers or where he went to get them, or the probable adventures he had doing so, is unrecorded. One wonders if he even received an apology for false imprisonment, or if he had not taken matters into his own hands by escaping and proving his own innocence.

The spring of 1779 probably saw numerous scouting parties sent out from the forts, but little is written about them. Timothy Murphy is said to have rescued the daughter of a man named Swart and killed four Indians doing so, at about this time. But, it is only one of the many unsubstantiated tales concerning that intrepid frontiersman.[71]

Despite the continual scouting and tough campaigns, there is no record of any casualties or men lost to the enemy for any reason during this period.

Destruction of the Iroquois Country

General Washington ordered the long awaited Indian expedition to be commanded by General John Sullivan who would bring up the main wing of the force from Pennsylvania. The northern force, under General James Clinton was to begin assembling in the Mohawk Valley. A smaller force under Colonel Daniel Brodhead would be launched from Fort Pitt and proceed up the Allegheny River.

Approximately 120 riflemen assembled at the Middle Fort on June 11, 1779, along with the 4th Pennsylvania. Some fifteen men with proper officers, from each regiment, remained at the fort in case of attack.[72]

The journal of Lieutenant Beatty, the officer of the 4th Pennsylvania, provides us with daily information on the rifle corps throughout the first part of the expedition. Leaving at 8 a.m. on June 11, Beatty's regiment and the rifle corps departed from the Middle Fort, and arrived at Schenectady at sundown and encamped, remaining there the following day. On the 13th, they crossed the Mohawk River and were supplied with 36 bateaux and provisions. The next day the men were greeted with showers and made only three miles upriver before encamping on shore. The rain continued into the night, making for "disagreeable" conditions in their tents. On June 15, ten more miles were made before again encamping on shore. On the 16th, the men made the thirteen miles to Major Jelles Fonda's residence, and on the 17th, made seventeen more miles to reach Canajoharie at sundown. Here they met Colonel Gansevoort's 3rd New York Regiment. After the boats were unloaded, the rifle corps encamped on the left of the New York troops.[73]

A look at the activities and duties of the riflemen at this time can be found in the order book of Captain Leonard Bleeker of the 3rd New York. While most of the troops were engaged in the laborious exercise of transporting the bateaux and supplies across the country to Otsego Lake, the duties of the rifle corps, while less exhausting perhaps, were much more dangerous as they "...will be employed in scouting the Woods and keeping up the Communications between the different Posts."[74] Together, the several regiments, the 2nd, 3rd, 4th and 5th, New York, 4th Pennsylvania, 6th Massachusetts, artillerymen, volunteers, and the rifle corps totaled about 1500 men, with about 220 bateaux.

LAKE OTSEGO FROM HYDE.

On June 19, some of the troops, including the rifle corps, reached the burned-out village of Springfield, after a 17-mile journey over a rough road. The men lay in camp on the 20th, but on the 21st, Major Parr with nearly 100 men was detached on a three-day scout to the south. Part of their mission was to clear out a part of the Susquehanna River and make it passable for boats. When Parr returned on June 23rd, he reported that the Susquehanna, of which he had gone down ten miles, was passable, but it was apparent the water level was daily lowering and within a short time the passage might become impossible for the heavily loaded bateaux. However, at a point ten miles below the river outlet Parr noted it was quite navigable because of the various springs and feeder streams. General Clinton sent two companies of the 6th Massachusetts to erect a dam across the outlet at the lower end of the lake,[75] in order to allow the water level to slowly rise.

On a warm and rainy June 25, "Capt. Simpson with 40 Rifle Men went on a scout; likewise Lieutenant Bevins with 20 Musket Men went on a scout,"[76] but returned on the 26th with no news.

It was on June 27, that one of the most remarkable individual feats of the rifle corps occurred while serving in upstate New York. David Ellerson related it to Simms more than half a century later. That the adventure happened, or at least, something very similar, is documented in the journals kept by Clinton's men.[77] Parties of Indians constantly skulked around the army, spying upon them from the neighboring mountains and providing the enemy with excellent intelligence daily. Brant had ordered his warriors to take a prisoner for intelligence.

On this day Ellerson was sent out by an officer to gather greens at a deserted farmhouse a mile or so away. While thus engaged, Ellerson set aside his rifle while he worked, as a dozen or so Indians attempted to slip up on him with their tomahawks, evidently with the intention of taking him alive. Upon seeing his intended captors, the "shirtman" snatched up his rifle and as he began to run, the Indians, fearing he might escape, hurled their tomahawks at him, one of which nearly severed a finger. The Indians now went back to their muskets and fired just as Ellerson plunged into the surrounding forest with the Indians in hot pursuit. Back at the camp the shots were heard and scouts were sent out, some believing he was taken, others that he must have been killed. Two journals state he lost his firearm, but Ellerson maintained to Simms that he carried his rifle throughout the ordeal. The rifleman was pursued mountain after mountain, stream after stream, hour after hour, as the wily Indians attempted to run down their equally crafty foe. Ellerson used every woodland stratagem to shake off pursuit, all to no avail, as the enemy kept doggedly on his trail. Finally, after perhaps 25 miles or more, Ellerson stopped, believing he had finally shaken off the Indians, when one appeared in front of him. Ellerson raised his rifle to bring him down, when a shot rang out behind him and entered his side just above the hip. He kept his feet, changed his course, and continued his flight, the enemy now closing in from two directions. Still he kept ahead of his pursuers, but after a mile and a half and feeling weak, he scooped up some water from a creek. He felt briefly invigorated, but with the loss of blood and exhaustion, he finally fell behind a log. He shot and killed the first warrior in sight. Sure of his own fate, he quickly reloaded and prepared to bring down another. The Indians, upon seeing their fallen comrade, stopped and curiously began weeping and singing. Having evidently killed their leader, Ellerson took advantage of the brief respite, withdrew deeper into the forest, lost his bloody trail in a winding stream, and crawled into a hollow log. The Indians may have continued their search, but if so, they failed to find their prey. Ellerson waited three days for the sun's rays to come out and direct his course towards the east. He made his way to Captain Christian Brown's residence near Cobleskill where he was cared for and sent back to the Middle Fort to recover.[78] In his pension account, Ellerson stated that he suffered long from his wound.[79] While novelists have him continuing on the expedition, it would seem that this was the end of it for him.

Meanwhile, the daily business of conducting scouts continued. Lieutenant Boyd took one out on June 29; Lieutenant Cotin went out with another the same day. On July 2, the troops marched passed Cherry Valley to Otsego Lake and then to its outlet at the southern end where they encamped to the right of George Croghan's house (Cooperstown). On July 4, Indians skulked about and fired at some sentries. At daybreak some of the men tracked a number of Indians. Parr and the riflemen again went out on scout that morning and thus missed a joyous celebration to commemorate the nation's third birthday. Lt. Elijah Evans, of Slaughter's Company, returned from a scout along the Susquehanna as far as "Yoackim's,"[80] about 20 miles downriver. On July 8, Colonel Butler and Major Parr were ordered to serve on a court-martial, while 50 riflemen were detached to guard a fatigue party.[81] The men had also been reviewed on July 6 by the adjutant general, and officers of all the regiments had been invited to a drink of grog.

A number of desertions occurred at about this time. On July 15, three men deserted from the 4th Pennsylvania. Some of these and others were caught and returned to camp to face punishment—often a whipping (one received 500 lashes) and sometimes death. The court-martial proceedings mention an interesting incident: three or four riflemen attempted to desert by crossing Otsego Lake in a boat, along with a soldier who claimed that he had not wanted to desert, but that the riflemen had turned their weapons on him and forced him to do so. The court did not accept this, and the man was promptly punished. The riflemen, it would seem, were never caught.

The troops found themselves battling boredom more than the enemy while the mundane activities of camp continued. On July 27, Major Parr became "Field Officer of the Day,"[82] and on August 1, half of the riflemen were paraded and given three days' provisions.[83] Major Parr went to Oak's Creek about three miles away with the cattle to pasture on this day, while other officers evidently met to learn the salute with the sword after which they were granted six kegs of rum. Some of the men still found time for their favorite avocation, as Lieutenant Beatty reported in his journal for August 3, the "Rifle men went down by the side of the lake to try their Rifles which they did by Shooting at marks."[84]

On August 4, the other half of the riflemen were paraded and given three days' provisions. Colonel Butler inspected their rifles. On August 7, the detachments were again paraded, given three days provisions and the advance troops were ordered to be commanded by Colonel Butler, Major Parr and Major Cochran, the latter of the 3rd New York regiment. The men were ordered to be ready, with their arms and ammunition well taken care of.[85]

The water had finally risen to a sufficient height and the dam was broken on August 9. Three men manned each bateau. In the plan of march, the rifle corps took the lead well in advance on the west side of the river, but were ordered not to quit sight of the boats if possible.[86] That day the troops marched 16 miles and made "Joachim's" the following day. The riflemen in front, the post of honor, sometimes found fresh Indian "sign," such as tracks, campfires, on one occasion a knife, etc.

A small Scotch settlement called "Albout" was burned on August 12. The troops then crossed to the east side at Unadilla and burned Glasford's house, as it was learned he had run off with the enemy. Here the Americans encamped on the site of their former triumph. The next day they recrossed to the west side and went to Conihunto, an Indian village.

The light troops went on two miles and encamped in the woods in advance of the main army. After passing Onoquaga, three Tuscarora towns were destroyed, among them Shawhiangto and Ingaren. Ingaren was located near present-day Great Bend, Pennsylvania. On August 18, Major Parr and 100

men went up the Chenango River to destroy the Indian town of Otsiningo (located about four miles north of present-day Binghamton, New York), but found it already burned, evidently by the enemy. Parr reported to General Clinton that the village had consisted of twenty hewn log houses and a few wigwams. Burning scattered huts and crops, Clinton's forces were met by two men from General Sullivan's wing. On the 20th, Owego was destroyed. A thousand-man detachment under General Enoch Poor was sent by Sullivan to meet General Clinton's force. Heavy rains prevented Clinton from Joining Sullivan immediately, but Clinton had sent out an express, headed by Lieutenant Boyd and nine other riflemen, to inform Sullivan that the union of the two forces had occurred and that they were presently enroute to the appointed rendezvous location at Tioga. Having left at 11 p.m. by boat, Boyd and his men made the best of their way down the river, and successfully completed the mission on the next day.[87]

August 22 saw Clinton's wing unite with that of Sullivan's, the combined force amounting to nearly 5000 men. Here, on the 23rd, the rifle corps was annexed to General Edward Hand's Brigade, which was to take the lead. This brigade was composed of the light infantry, the 4th Pennsylvania, the rifle corps and any volunteers. However, the riflemen were to be considered a separate corps, "As there are four Cos. Of Light Infantry annexed to Butler's, the rifle corps together with such other Rifle Men, as may be added to them, are to be a separate Corps and kept advanced of the army as General Hand may direct."[88] A militia rifle company from Pennsylvania, under Captain Schott, was added. Among the volunteers, mainly civilian riflemen, was Moses Van Campen. From Northumberland, Pennsylvania, Van Campen would later dictate his memoirs to his biographer, leaving us a detailed description of this campaign. All told, the number of riflemen and volunteers probably totaled something in the neighborhood of 175 to 200.

When the united forces began to pull out, it was "...the rifle Men in front of the whole reconoiting Mountains, roads, Defiles, etc," while the light infantry came next in six columns, each column two deep and two or three hundred yards distant from each other, the rest of the army in their appointed positions.[89] Lieutenant Colonel Adam Hubley noted that the riflemen were "...to prevent any surprise or ambuscade from taking place."[90]

Supplies were, as usual, slow in arriving and an officer wrote "...the men are poorly clothed and not above one in 10 have a blanket...," but such conditions were nothing new to these experienced, veteran Continentals.

There is one of those numerous tales concerning Timothy Murphy, which supposedly happened at about this time. Sent out on a scout (including Joseph Evans, Zachariah Tufts, and Joachim Folluck), Murphy espied an Indian in a canoe on the Chemung River, and though the target was at great distance, so great that the other riflemen thought it impossible, Murphy was determined to try. One shot and Murphy had his man.[91] Just another unlikely tale? Perhaps, yet the journals make mention of an incident on August 23. Sergeant Nathaniel Webb wrote, "One of our scouting parties killed and scalped an Indian five miles up the West Branch" of the

Chemung River.[92] Another entry for that day reported the killing, adding that the scout brought the victim's body back to camp.

A fort consisting of a stockade and blockhouses was constructed at Tioga and named after General Sullivan. From here the troops moved out on August 26, the riflemen in the manner aforesaid. On the 27th, the pioneers, who were to clear the way for the army, went to the "Narrow" near Newtown to mend and cut a road "...under cover of the rifle corps."[93] On that day, a scout was sent out and reported a large number of fires seen, that the enemy was formidable, ready to give battle, and that four or five enemy scouting parties were detected.[94] In his biography, Van Campen claimed to have been on this rather useful, informative scout, which returned on the 28th. Major Parr, in advance, had also seen a number of fires, as well as several Indians.

On the morning of August 29, Major Parr advanced cautiously with his riflemen. Several small groups of Indians were seen ahead and fired a few harmless shots. The major, however, knew better than to send his men ahead in pursuit. When they reached an area cleared of trees near the Chemung River, with mountains on the other sides, it seemed to Parr the perfect place for an ambush. Parr was a half mile ahead of General Hand, who in turn was a mile and a half in advance of the main army.

Although all this time the Indians had become bolder and more frequently seen, Parr's men still withheld their fire. At

11 a.m., when all was suspiciously quiet, Parr sent a rifleman up a tree, who, after some time, spotted the enemy behind breastworks artfully covered with the branches of trees. It was the bright vermilion war paint of the Indians that gave them away. Parr reported it to Hand, who ordered the major to take his men and advance on a position directly beneath the west bank of Baldwin Creek, only about 120 yards from the enemy. Here the riflemen opened fire.

The enemy force consisted of about 700 or 800 men, mainly Col. John Butler's Rangers, Joseph Brant's Iroquois warriors, and a small detachment of British regulars. The "Rifle Corp and the Indians made great halooing..."[95] as the former kept up a "scattering" fire to amuse the enemy while the army formed for battle. A surveyor for the Americans mentioned Parr's "...Core of Riflemen, who did Considerable Execution."[96]

Parties of the enemy were sent out on feints towards the riflemen to draw them in, but these veteran soldiers with their intrepid commanders, would not fall so easily a prey. At one time, some 400 Indians sallied out "...But finding our troops determined to maintain their positions returned to their works."[97]

After the American force was deployed, the riflemen were withdrawn from their position along the creek and attached to General Poor's brigade. The Americans soon encountered thick underbrush as they made a circuit around the enemy's flank. When they reached the mountain on the right, the Indian war whoop was sounded and "The riflemen kept up a scattering fire," while "...we formed the Line of Battle, then we advanced with Fixed Bayonets without Firing a Shot altho they kept up a Steady fire upon the whole of the way up the Hill, Which is about Half a mile."[98] Here the fighting was the most severe, the flanking brigade suffering many of the American casualties. The riflemen could scatter ahead of Poor's regulars, but by themselves could not have held back the enemy. It is possible to perceive that if the more heavily laden soldiers could have adapted the tactics and movements of the riflemen, the enemy force might have been taken or destroyed. As it was, Poor's men were too slow, for when the artillery opened fire, the Indians panicked and fled, escaping by the route Poor's brigade would have blocked.

Still, the riflemen and light infantry, with seemingly boundless energy, pursued the retreating foe "...about 3 miles so as to oblige Enemy to Leave a Great part of their Packs, etc."[99] The advance troops saw the Indians, along with their wounded, frantically make their escape in canoes up the Chemung. The riflemen, in this latter part of the action, captured a black ranger.

Thanks to the rifle corps, the army had been spared what could have been a devastating ambuscade. It had been the rifle corps that initiated the fighting and it had been the rifle corps and light infantry that were the last to break off the action.

For such a ferocious fight, casualties were rather low: about three killed and 39 wounded for the Americans. About twelve Indians were found dead on the field and considerable numbers of others, along with the wounded, were reported carried off. Among the Loyalists, we can only say several were killed or wounded, as Col. John Butler's estimates of his losses cannot be taken as factual. Two prisoners were taken, one of them the black previously mentioned. An enemy officer stated the Loyalist loss as being a total of 13, including the captured. That night, the exhausted riflemen camped in a cornfield before returning to the army the following day.

On August 31, the enemy was discovered going up the main branch of the Tioga River in boats and canoes. Colonel Dayton's 3rd New Jersey, Butler's 4th Pennsylvania and the rifle corps were dispatched after them, but did not manage to make contact with them. Another night, a miserable one, was spent in another cornfield before the troops returned at 10 a.m. on September 1. Before returning, they burned a number of houses and destroyed the corn.[100]

From 11 a.m. until 9:30 p.m., the American army thrashed and slogged its way through a six-mile hemlock swamp on the approach to Catherine's Town. Catherine's Town was named for Catherine Montour, sister of the notorious half-blood Indian woman, Esther Montour, who was guilty of atrocities in the Wyoming valley the year before. As they neared the town the howling of dogs and other noises could be heard. "A few of the riflemen were dispatched in order to reconnoiter the place...," and returned to say it was abandoned.[101] On the 2nd, a small scout reconnoitered the woods and claimed to have discovered the enemy some eight miles away.[102] At noon, Colonel William Butler, with 300 or

400 men, went out in search of some squaws and children, but found none.[103]

A rare Iroquois-built log cabin built of hewn logs neatly dovetailed at the corners and as skillfully done as many white settlers' homes. With its bark roof and gables it very closely fits the descriptions of the cabins burnt down during the Sullivan-Clinton campaign in 1779. Photo courtesy of Richard J. Whalen.

As the army made its way along the shores of Seneca Lake, all towns and cultivated fields were put to the torch. Upon entering the town of Kendian of the 5th, the riflemen retook Luke Swetland, who provided information that the Indians intended to make another stand, perhaps at Canandaigua. A shot was fired from the nearby woods which knocked a stick out of one man's hand, but the assailant escaped.[104] The troops approached Kanadasage (site of present-day Geneva) slowly and with caution. As the riflemen and light infantry crossed the mouth of the lake, "...about knee deep and not above thirty yards wide," they entered three dangerous defiles reckoned as good ambuscade points, but no attack came.[105]

At 10 a.m., on September 8, Major Parr and the rifle corps took a cohorn, and along with several other parties, were dispatched 8 miles down the lake to burn "Kushay." Here 15 log houses were burned, 5 horses were taken, and extensive crops were discovered on the banks of the lake. Evidently, a very large longhouse, or a "bark hutt," was left standing under which all of the men spent the night. Crops were so extensive here that Parr requested reinforcements. When some 200 more men arrived, the destruction was complete and the rifle corps returned to the main army on the ninth.[106]

Because supplies were getting dangerously low, the troops were put on half-rations, which was accepted with spirit by the men. Lieutenant Beatty wrote, "...hungry bellies and hard duty... which I think we may call hard times." Many of the soldiers also began to wonder why the feared Iroquois, their homeland being overrun and destroyed, were not attempting another stand, or even attempting to slow down or hinder the advance. Although the Indians were outnumbered some 6 or 7 to one, "...a few men of spirit, might exceedingly retard our movements."[107]

The American army now left Seneca Lake and began to travel through the wilderness toward the Genesee River. The riflemen were usually the first to enter each town, and upon entering Hanyaye, or Honeyoye, the Indians quickly fled, leaving "Packs & Blankets & potatoes Roasting in the fire."[108]

It was from the area of ground later known as Henderson's Flats, near the head of Conesus Lake, that General Sullivan gave Lt. Thomas Boyd verbal instructions to take five or six riflemen and attempt to find an Indian town situated near the Genesee. Instead of taking the number stated, Boyd took a number of volunteers, totaling about 28 men. Lieutenant Beatty said this scout was composed of 18 riflemen and 8 musketmen (there were also 2 Indian guides), but others give numbers of about half and half. We shall probably never know as history has not recorded all of their names.

Leaving on September 13, the scout found the town of "Gaghsuquiluher" evacuated, which they had mistaken for Little Beard's town. At daybreak, Boyd sent his runners back to inform Sullivan and then retired a little into the woods to watch and try to take a prisoner. Four Indians rode in on horseback and Boyd ordered five or six men to kill or take them. However, only one was killed and another wounded, Murphy being the one who killed the Indian. Murphy ran up and scalped his fallen foe, this being his 33rd kill of the war so far. He also supplanted his own moccasins with those of the Indian's, to which he took a liking. Boyd sent two more runners to the army, but they soon returned and informed him they had seen five Indians on the road. Alarmed, Boyd knew he must return before the enemy discovered his whereabouts. On the return trip, Boyd's forward scouts began to see Indians and began to give chase. Two riflemen in front fired simultaneously at an Indian and killed him. As they began to argue over the scalp, the woods became alive with hundreds of Tories and Indians.[109] It has become evident that the real design of the enemy was to ambush the main army, but Boyd's blundering scout changed the enemy's plan. Hearing the firing to the rear, and believing themselves attacked from that direction, Butler and Brant immediately rushed there with their men. Boyd's men were "...obliged to attempt a retreat, at the same time loading and firing as his party ran."[110] The flankers did the only thing they could do under the circumstances—they ran. Some were pursued and outran the enemy to the American camp. A few hid themselves in the woods and witnessed the action.

Boyd and his men took refuge, about 16 or 17 strong, on a small knoll surrounded by an open meadow. This gave them the advantage of a clear field of fire, but outnumbered some 25 to 1, the men had little hope. It is said that the cornered Americans actually threw back the enemy three times, or attempted to break through as many times, but the battle lasted only a few minutes as the horde of rangers and Indians swarmed over the knoll. In a swirl of clubbed rifles, thrusting bayonets, and swinging tomahawks, the inevitable end soon came. Only Boyd and one of the riflemen, Michael Parker,[111] were spared. In a rage, Hanyerry, a faithful Oneida chief, found with the Americans, was killed, his body literally cut to pieces.

The scouts who were so hotly pursued, approached the American camp. A surveying party in advance, seeing the Indians in pursuit, dropped their instruments and also fled for their lives. An alert sentry shot one of the Indians. Almost immediately the rifle corps and light infantry, under Hand, were dispatched. So quickly were they upon the scene of action that the enemy, taken by surprise, fled the field without firing a shot, leaving a multitude of equipment behind. Hand's troops now gained a booty of 100 blankets, 70 packs, kettles and other goods.[112] Those hiding in the woods came forth and survivors, including the two runners, probably numbered some nine or eleven men out of the 28. They said "...that the party ware surrounded, But fought and Retreted & Killed several, they think as many as ware Lost of our side,"

and that "...from Circumstance it appeared they had Defended Them selves very Bravely till they ware all kild, and it is thought Kild a nomber of the Enemy, as many fresh Indian Graves were found at Chenassee—some ware opanid by the Soldiers Contrary to orders, and Boadies of Indians found that ware shot..."[113] Other corpses had been found burned in a house at this village as well. Lt. Col. Henry Dearborn wrote that Boyd's men were determined to sell their lives dearly and fought until all were killed.[114] The enemy's casualties will probably never be ascertained but we do know the names of some of the Americans killed and others who escaped. Those slain were Thomas Boyd, John Conroy, Benjamin Curtin, James McElboy, William Harvey, Nicholas Hungerman, John Millers, Michael Parker, John Putnam, Corporal William Faughey, Corporal Thomas McElwayn, Corporal John Callaghan and Hanyerry (the Oneida chief). Those who escaped were Timothy Murphy, Edward McDonald, John Salmon, Garret Putman, John Youse and Captain Jehoiakim (a Stockbridge Indian).[115]

Boyd and Parker were taken to Chenussio (or Little Beard's Town), on the Genesee and were interrogated by Colonel John Butler. Nineteenth-century historians were fond of such terms as "heroic," "gallant," "noble," etc., when describing Boyd and how he supposedly preferred death to corroborating with the "bloodthirsty" Butler. Actually, Boyd did talk, as shown in a letter from Butler to Lt. Col. Bolton, dated September 14. "The Officer who is a very intelligent Person Says, their Army consists of near 5000 Continental Troops—1500 of which are Rifle Men, commanded by General Sullivan and Brigadiers Hand, Poor and Clinton. They have but a month's Provisions, and intend, according to his account, to come no further than Genesse—They have four Pieces of Cannon (the largest a Six Pounder) a Cohorn and a Howitzer-They are building a strong Fort at Tioga and mean to keep a large Garrison there."[116] Perhaps it is to

Boyd's credit that he multiplied the number of riflemen some ten times their actual number, but there can be no doubt that the officer referred to was he.

A view of Fort Niagara. It was from this post that raiding parties of Indians and Loyalist rangers were sent out to attack the frontiers of New York and Pennsylvania. Photo by the author.

It is questionable whether Butler then turned his captives over to the Indians for torture, although a woman captive from that town did claim this to have been so. It might well have been that after Butler and Brant departed for Fort Niagara, the Indians lost no time in pouncing upon the prisoners. The Senecas had seen their land overrun and destroyed and now took their vengeance out on these riflemen.

On September 14, the advancing army locked arms to cross the Genesee River, which was running swiftly at this point, and soon entered upon a beautiful plain where Little Beard's Town was situated. Among the first to find the mutilated remains of Boyd and Parker was Moses Van Campen. John Salmon, one of Boyd's riflemen, and later a pioneer settler of Avon, N.Y., left an interesting account of his experiences on this campaign. All those who kept journals vividly described the abuses heaped upon Boyd and Parker.

"At this place we found the body of the brave but unfortunate Lieutenant Boyd, and one rifleman, massacred in the most cruel and barbarous manner that the human mind can possibly conceive; the savages having put them to the most excruciating torments possible, by first plucking their nails from their hands, then spearing, cutting, and whipping them, and mangling their bodies, then cutting off the flesh from their shoulders by piece, tomahawking and severing their heads from their bodies, and then leaving them prey to their dogs. We likewise found one house burned, in which, probably, was a scene as cruel as the former.

"This evening the remains of Lieutenant Boyd and the rifleman's corpse were interred with military honors. Mr. Boyd's former good character, as a brave soldier, and an honest man, and his behaviour in the skirmish of yesterday (several of the Indians being found dead, and some seen carried off,) must endear him to all friends of mankind. May his fate await those who have been the cause of his."[117]

The bodies were interred with full military honors by Captain Simpson's company of riflemen, and the spot, at the juncture of Boyd and Parker Creeks, was remembered by the early settlers. Curiosity seekers among the latter are said to have exhumed the remains of Boyd's men, taking parts of their clothing and buttons.[118] In 1841, a ceremony with great fanfare took place, and the remains of the men were reinterred at Mount Hope Cemetery in Rochester.[119] There, a monument to these fallen heroes can be seen today.

An ancient oak tree, called the "Torture Tree" still stands, said to be the one by which Boyd and Parker were slain.

A doctor with the army wrote, "The Indians are exceedingly dirty, the rubage of one of their houses is enough to stink a whole country," when he was at Little Beard's

Town.[120] This was one of the largest and most prosperous of the Indian towns, and while the rifle corps and a detachment from each brigade stood guard, the whole army turned out to destroy the town and crops. Because of the lack of supplies and the lateness of the season, General Sullivan abandoned the goal of capturing Fort Niagara and ordered the army to begin its homeward march. Recrossing the Genesee,

the rifle corps again had the post of honor, that of being the last to cross and covering the rear in case of attack. On September 16, the ambuscade site was passed, and the bodies of the men interred. They were found "...scalped, tomahawked, and most inhumanly mangled."[121]

At Canandaigua, a council was held with the Oneidas who had accompanied the army. They asked that the Cayugas, who they believed had not been responsible for attacking the frontiers, be spared the destruction of their towns. The American officers were not convinced and a detachment was ordered out to destroy the Cayuga towns and crops, and that all males were to be treated as prisoners of war. Some 600 men, including the rifle corps and the 4th Pennsylvania, under the command of Colonel Butler, were dispatched from Canadasaga (Geneva) at 3 p.m. on September 20.

This detachment went eight miles to Scawyace or "Long Falls" (site of present-day Waterloo), as they followed the Seneca River. Here a most unique display of Indian ingenuity was discovered. Circular stone enclosures 30 or 40 feet in diameter were built up on the rocky bed of a stream, where the water was not deep or fast, so as to permit water to pass through while retaining fish. This town of 18 houses was burned.[122]

The next day the troops marched at 7 a.m. and made 16½ miles to Gewanga, crossed the outlet of Cayuga Lake which was mid-deep and destroyed Choharo at the foot of the lake on the east side. The road was never more than a half mile from the lake.[123]

On September 22, Cayuga Castle (site of present-day Springport), a town of 15 large houses of squared logs, was burned. Here beef was found and issued. Also found were some salt springs, and importantly, muskets branded U.S. and blue regimental coats faced with white.[124] Two other towns, Upper Cayuga (14 houses) and East Cayuga (13 houses) were found this day and destroyed on the following day. On the 23rd, the march continued for five more miles and the town of Chondote, 14 houses, (site of present-day Aurora), was found. On the 24th this town was destroyed along with 1500 peach trees. That night the Americans encamped on "Pleasant Hill" (north of present-day Ludlowville) after making 16 or 17 miles. Two noteworthy waterfalls were passed, one 80 feet high (probably on Mill Creek, 2½ miles southwest of Northville), and the other about 50 feet high[125] (near Lake Ridge in present-day Lansing). On the 25th through the 27th, the men passed through the "Great Swamp" and on the 27th they steered by the sun alone, there being no path or road. On the 28th they rejoined the main army.[126] Colonel Butler used the captured muskets, along with some scalps, to show the Oneidas that the Cayugas had, to some degree, been hostile towards the Americans. All told, Butler's expedition destroyed five towns, 200 acres of corn and over 1500 fruit trees.

During the entire expedition over 40 Indian towns had been destroyed, including about 1200 houses, in each of which 2 or 3 or more families sometimes lived. Some 200,000 bushels of corn, 50,000 bushels of potatoes, beans, squash and other vegetables were destroyed and 10,000 fruit trees cut down or girdled. It was thought the great Iroquois Confederacy was humbled, but with British support they would continue their raids with even greater ferocity, vengeance paving the way.

Many of the soldiers of this expedition saw the great richness and fertility of the soil and returned after the war. Among the riflemen, Moses Van Campen, William Leek and John Salmon settled in that area.

The return trip followed Sullivan's march up—via the Susquehanna River, the Wyoming Valley and finally Easton. On November 19, while at Pompton, New Jersey, the rifle corps and the 6th Massachusetts were ordered to West Point, but were detained for want of wagons until the 12th when they traveled to Ramapo, New York. The next day they made 17 miles, only 2 miles from King's Ferry. On November 14, they crossed at the ferry, scene of the night assault on Stony Point and recently abandoned by the British, over to Peekskill. On November 15, they crossed the Hudson River again and arrived at West Point.[127]

Washington had already issued orders for the disbandment of these last two companies of Morgan's elite rifle corps. On November 9, the following general orders were given; "The officers & privates Composing the Rifle Corps under the Command of Major Parr are all to join their respective Regts. The Major will see that all the Rifles & their

Proper Bullet Moulds etc. are Collected & Numbered to prevent their being Separated & have them delivered to the Commissary of Military Stores & take his Receipt. The commissary is to see the Rifles etc. to be Carefully Box'd up & is not to deliver any of them without an order from the Commander in Chief. Muskets are to be drawn for the Men in Lieu of their Rifles.

"The Gen'l. Cannot dissolve this Corps without returning his particular thanks to the Officer & Soldiers remaining in it for their long faithful & Important Services."[128]

Thus was accomplished with a pen what the enemy had never been able to do with the sword. Except for a small detachment of riflemen at Fort Pitt, there were practically none left in the Continental Army, notwithstanding their battle record. Ironically, some of the greatest moments of the war were yet to be won by militia riflemen in the south.

Morgan's Riflemen had left their mark, both on the American and British armies. Not long after the war both nations adopted rifle regiments as part of their armies. The British historian Trevelyan stated that these riflemen of Morgan's were possibly, the best regiment, man for man, in military history, with the possible exception of a British regiment that served in the Napoleonic Wars.[129]

The Schoharie Valley had not seen the last of these men. At least 10 returned in late 1779 and early 1780, enlisted in the local militia, served for the most part as Rangers, and become folk heroes to the people of the area. Schoharie has every reason to be proud of that elite corps of riflemen who served her so valiantly.

Part Two

The Officers

Thomas Posey (1750 - 1818)

Perhaps one of the most important men ever to serve in Schoharie was Thomas Posey. Born on July 9, 1750, in Fairfax County, Virginia, Thomas spent his boyhood in a rural environment enjoying few educational advantages. His mother was Elizabeth Lloyd, of a family of high social standing. Incredibly, he is said to have been the illegitimate son of none other than George Washington himself, who, it has been supposed, never had any natural children.[130]

Evidently searching for adventure, Thomas headed for the frontier and settled in the new county of Botetourt, Virginia. He was commissary-general under General Andrew Lewis and served in the battle with the Indians at Point Pleasant (present-day West Virginia) on October 10, 1774. It was in this bloody engagement that the Shawnee Indians were defeated by an army of backwoods riflemen, or the "Long Knives," who inflicted one of the few, and certainly the worst, defeat yet suffered by the Indians in an open, woodland battle. It was a feat of a scale never achieved by the professional, well-trained armies of Europe.

Commissioned by Congress as captain, Posey raised his own company and joined the 7th Virginia, and participated in the campaign that, with the successful action at Gwynn's Island, drove Lord Dunmore out of Virginia. Marching to Washington's encampment at Middlebrook, New Jersey, in early 1777, Posey had the honor to be selected one of the captains in Colonel Daniel Morgan's new rifle corps. Jared Sparks, who wrote a biography of Posey commented, "The corps soon became one of the most distinguished in the army; its hard and continual service, and brilliant successes, showed not only that its energies were directed by a master spirit, but that all its parts were composed of stern and war-like materials. It was immediately ordered to do duty on the enemy's lines, where it was much exposed, always on the alert, and frequently engaged with the enemy's picket guards, their foraging parties, or some part of their forces. To say that on these occasions Captain Posey was not excelled by any of the brave officers of this gallant regiment, is high praise, but it may be said with strict justice." When General Howe evacuated New Brunswick and directed his march for New York, Morgan's riflemen hung onto the rear of the enemy, attempting to engage at every defile, generally harassing the British at every opportunity. When the enemy force reached Piscataway, Morgan, who had his men posted in a marshy wood near the road, waited in silence until the main body of the enemy passed, and then dashed upon the rear guard. While this action was taking place, Posey was ordered, with his company, to cross a causeway leading through a swamp in order to gain the front of the portion of the enemy engaged and cut it off from the main body. This was accomplished, but Posey soon found himself nearly surrounded by the light troops of the enemy and nearly cut off. Perceiving this, Posey concentrated the rifle fire of his company at a particular point of the enemy's force, literally blew open an escape route, charged through gallantly, and thus effected a retreat. Posey's company suffered most of the casualties in this otherwise successful action. His unit also was present at the two battles of Saratoga, which culminated in Burgoyne's surrender. While most of the Continental Army spent the winter of 1777-1778 at Valley Forge, portions of the rifle corps were stationed at Radnor, near the lines of the British forces then in possession of Philadelphia. Upon Morgan's return home on furlough, Lt. Col. Richard Butler having joined his original regiment, and Major Morris having been recently killed, Captain Posey succeeded to the command of the rifle corps. After seeing so much arduous service, hardships and privation, the rifle corps was now much reduced in strength. Winter was no respite for these troops and they continued to perform the active duties of the partisan service. The following spring and early summer, with the corps again commanded by Morgan, Posey saw more action in Pennsylvania and New Jersey.

In July 1778, Posey, now "captain-commandant," again found himself in charge of the remains of the rifle corps: six companies having been disbanded and only the companies of Captains Gabriel Long and James Parr left intact. These, a little over 100 strong, along with Lt. Col. William Butler's 4th Pennsylvania, were detached to the Schoharie frontier to defend the settlers against the frequent incursions of the Loyalists and Indians, and if possible, to carry the war into their own country. Posey's activities at this time, gleaned largely from the papers of Governor George Clinton, demonstrate how Posey's character was held in high esteem by those who knew him.

His tour of duty was brief in Schoharie, but included involvement with the successful Onoquaga-Unadilla Campaign. In a letter dated December 20, 1778, Washington ordered Posey, now a major, to return to the 7th Virginia. In his stead, Parr was promoted to command of the riflemen in Schoharie.

Rejoining Washington at Middlebrook, New Jersey, Major Posey was later selected for the "Corps of Light Infantry," an elite force commanded by General Anthony Wayne. In the daring and successful midnight assault on Stony Point, on July 15, 1779, Posey displayed great bravery. One hundred and fifty volunteers, led by Lt. Col. Fluery and Major Posey, formed the advance of the right column and rushed to the assault with unloaded muskets and fixed bayonets. Fluery is said to have been the first to strike the British standard. Major Posey, mounting the works almost at the same instant was the first to give the watchword, "The fort's our own." By making a successful charge on a battery of two 24-pound pieces, Posey helped silence the part of the enemy's stronghold that had been firing on the left column.

After having narrowly missed being a part of the American force that surrendered at Charleston, South Carolina, Posey was present at the surrender at Yorktown. In 1781-1782, he was ordered to join General Wayne in Georgia. During the night attack by the Creek Indians under Gueristersigo, Posey distinguished himself by bringing order out of confusion and helping to save the main body, killing several of the enemy with his own sword. On September 8, 1782, he was promoted to the rank of lieutenant-colonel. He retired from the service on March 10, 1783.

After the war, Posey settled in Spotsylvania County, Virginia, and became county lieutenant and magistrate. On February 14, 1793, he became a brigadier general and served, once again, under his friend and fellow soldier, General Wayne, in the old Northwest. He seems to have returned to the east before the decisive battle of Fallen Timbers and resigned on February 28, 1794. At the close of the Indian war he settled in Kentucky and was elected to the state senate. He was lieutenant-governor and speaker from 1805 to 1806. When war threatened with Great Britain or France in 1809, Posey was assigned to the command of Volunteers with the rank of major-general. When the War of 1812 broke out, General Posey, then living in the Attakapas region of Louisiana, immediately raised a company of available men and willingly became their captain, although holding a major-general's commission, but is not credited with active military service. He was appointed to fill a vacancy in the U.S. Senate in 1812, until that position expired, whereupon President Madison appointed him governor of the Indiana territory. He served in that post until it became a state in 1816. As a candidate for the first governorship of the state, he was defeated by Jonathan Jennings. In 1817, he lost the election for representative to Congress. He was appointed Indian agent in 1816, an office he held until his death at Shawneetown, Illinois, on March 19, 1818.

General Posey was the very opposite of the stereotypical image of the illiterate, uncouth, rollicking frontiersman. After his term of office as governor, the territorial legislature addressed him as follows: "They cannot refrain from declaring their perfect approbation of your official conduct as Governor of this territory. During your administration, many evils have been remedied, and we particularly admire the calm, dispassionate, impartial conduct, which has produced the salutary effects of quieting the violence of party spirit, harmonizing the interests, as well as the feelings, of the different parties of the territory. Under your auspices we have become as one people."[131]

James Parr (died before 1804)

James Parr, who rose to the rank of major and became well known as one of the most intrepid of the rifle commanders, has left us with virtually no record of his life subsequent to the Revolution. He was from Buffalo Valley, near New Columbia, and became first lieutenant in Captain John Lowdon's Company of Thompson's Rifle Battalion, raised in June of 1775, in Sunbury, Pennsylvania. The privates were from the West Branch valley of the Susquehanna, around and north of Sunbury, and in the Northumberland area. Among these men were a number who would become noted riflemen including Samuel Brady, Timothy Murphy, Peter Pence, and William Leek, among others. This company of 97 men, uniting with several others, were among the first troops outside of New England to arrive at Cambridge to join Washington's army, making the march from Pennsylvania in near record time to arrive there on August 9.[132]

Nearly 900 strong, Thompson's Rifle Battalion formed the picket guard for some 2000 Provincials who took possession of, and then threw up entrenchments on Ploughed Hill on August 16, and on the following day suffered its first casualties.

On October 24, a detachment from Lowdon's company marched from Prospect Hill, near Cambridge. Lieutenant Colonel Hand wrote, "An officer, Parr, from Northumberland, with thirty men from us, marched from Portsmouth. They marched at dawn this morning."[133] On November 9, Lowdon's company was in a skirmish at Lechmere's Point. In this action, nine companies of British light infantry, and 100 grenadiers landed on the point to seize cattle needed for the Boston garrison. Thompson's Battalion counterattacked and plunged, with spirit, through two feet of icy water, advanced on the enemy and forced them to retreat. The British loss was 17 killed and 2 wounded, as compared to 2 Americans wounded. The extremely high ratio of killed to wounded indicates the riflemen were aiming for sure kills.[134]

On January 1, 1776, Colonel Thompson's battalion of riflemen became the "First Regiment" of the Continental Line, also known as the 1st Pennsylvania, and on February 2, Colonel Hand assumed command. The Battle of Dorchester Heights took place on March 4, and on March 9, Parr succeeded Lowdon as captain. On March 14, Parr's company left Cambridge with Hand's First Pennsylvania along with five other regiments under General Sullivan to prevent a British landing at New York, where it was believed the enemy would go after abandoning Boston on March 17. Parr's company arrived at Hartford on March 21, and at New York on the 28th. They then were stationed on Long Island. Colonel Hand's riflemen remained in the area, picketing the shores of the island until August, when they were transferred to Delancey's Mills, three miles above King's Bridge. So successful were the riflemen in opposing and retarding the landing enemy troops that the Hessian, or German, officers made a formal complaint about their "unfair" method of carrying on a war. After five days of incessant scouting and skirmishing, the battalion was withdrawn just before the battle of Long Island on August 27, 1776, and thus escaped that disaster intact. It is ironic that the enemy took its revenge upon Colonel Miles' Pennsylvania State Rifle Battalion. After the fall of Forts Washington and Lee, Washington retreated across New Jersey before falling upon the Germans at Trenton on December 26. In this daring strike, Hand's riflemen further distinguished themselves when they led the advance, and again when they helped slow down Cornwallis's whole army during the daylight hours of January 2, 1777. They also played a prominent role in the victory at Princeton the following day.

When Morgan's famed rifle corps was formed in the spring of 1777, Parr found himself on detached duty as captain of the sixth company of eight. Colonel James Chambers, who succeeded Hand as colonel of the First Pennsylvania, wrote the latter from Mount Prospect Park camp in New Jersey on June 18: "We have a partizan Regt.–Col. Morgan commands–Chosen Marksmen from the Whole Army Composing it. Capt. Parr, Lt. Lyon & Brady, & Fifty men from my Regt. Are amongst the number..."[135] Captain David Harris wrote from Cross Roads, near Philadelphia on August 13, to General Hand: "Col. Butler, Captain Parr, with two subalterns, and about 50 privates, are detached in Morgan's Partizan Corps. Captain Parr has killed three or four men himself this summer. His expressions at the Death of one I shall ever Remember. Major Miller had the Command of a Detachment, and had a skirmish at very close shot with a Party of Highlanders. One of them being quite open, he motioned to Capt. Parr to kill him, which he did in a thrice, and, as he was falling, Parr said: 'I say, by God, Sawny, I am in you.' I assure Parr's bravery on every occasion does him great Honour."[136]

Parr further saw action during the Saratoga Campaign, where, although little is known of his personal exploits, it was one of his men, Timothy Murphy, who is credited with shooting British General Simon Fraser at the Battle of Bemis Heights, on October 7, 1777, thus helping to turn the tide of battle.

After the encampment at Valley Forge, during which the rifle corps had been so active, Parr's company further distinguished itself. On May 18, 1778, Washington sent Lafayette as an advance guard between the Schuylkill and the Delaware to watch for the expected British evacuation of Philadelphia. Clinton attempted to capture Lafayette's force, but the latter made a skillful retreat across Matson's Ford on the Schuylkill River. Parr and his men were a few hundred yards in advance of Lafayette's left wing.

Shortly after the battle of Monmouth, six of the eight companies of Morgan's regiment were disbanded, the men returning to the regiments from which they were originally drafted. Only the companies of Captains Parr and Long were left intact, and these, along with Colonel William Butler's 4th Pennsylvania, were detached to the Schoharie frontier. Captain Commandant Thomas Posey commanded the "remains" of the rifle corps. On October 9, Parr was promoted to major of the 7th Pennsylvania, but was still on detached duty with the rifle corps. Upon the absence of Posey shortly thereafter, Parr assumed command of the rifle corps. Participating in the expeditions against Unadilla and Onoquaga during that same month, Parr's men performed heroically. Colonel Butler sent Parr out with a party three miles lower down the Susquehanna to burn an Indian (Tuscarora) village, and to deceive the enemy by a feigned pursuit. Some of Parr's riflemen, under Lieutenant Elijah Evans, were detached up the Mohawk Valley and took part in the Van Schaik raid on the Onondagas in April 1779.

Parr's greatest achievement was in his skilled and expert handling of the rifle corps during the Sullivan-Clinton expedition. In June 1779, he took out a scout to the southern end of Otsego Lake and discovered the water depth would soon make it impossible to float bateaux down the Susquehanna River. A dam was soon constructed to remedy this problem. His men led the advance of the army and when they went to destroy the town of Otstiningo, near present-day Binghamton, found it to have been already burned and abandoned by the enemy. His behavior and the expertise of his troops helped prevent what could have been a devastating ambuscade near Newtown on August 29. It was Parr's riflemen who usually led the advance into each Indian town. His regiment was again under Colonel Butler in the destruction of the Cayuga towns in September 1779. Ordered to West Point, at the conclusion of the campaign, the rifle corps was disbanded by General Washington's order in November. However, in July of 1780, a small detachment of riflemen was drafted together from some Pennsylvania regiments and served briefly under Parr.[137] Some of these men may have been from the Schoharie detachment. According to a resolution of Congress effective January 17, 1781, the quota of Pennsylvania was reduced and Major James Parr was retired as of that date.[138]

Little is known of Parr's post-war life, but it is believed he died before 1804.

Michael Simpson (1733 ? - 1813)

"Here, my dear children, permit me to give you the genuine character of my friend, general Simpson, whom you all know personally. He was among my earliest and best friends. He was then as apparently eccentric, as he is at this time: there is no obvious difference in his manners between the two periods. As an officer, he was always active and keen in the performance of his duty. Hard was the service; but his heart was soft to his friend." Published in Lancaster in 1812, this excerpt is from John Joseph Henry's vivid account of the Quebec campaign. From this, as well as references from several other sources, a quantity of information has come to light regarding this rifle officer.

Evidently from the area of Paxton, Pennsylvania, Simpson was chosen as lieutenant in Captain Matthew Smith's company of Thompson's Rifle Battalion. It is believed that many of Smith's men had been members of the notorious "Paxton Boys," a group of vigilantes responsible for the murder of the Conestoga Indians and causing other upheavals on the Pennsylvania frontier in the 1760's. While Henry condemned Smith for his major role in the killings, he made no reference to his friend Simpson, of whom he thought highly, as having been a member of the gang. Smith's company made the march to Cambridge in the summer of 1775, where, posted outside of the besieged city of Boston, they wreaked great havoc with their sharpshooting upon the British.

In September, three rifle companies were chosen to lead the expeditionary force to capture Quebec, under Colonel Benedict Arnold. These companies were captained by William Hendricks of Carlisle, Pennsylvania, Daniel Morgan of Winchester, Virginia, and Matthew Smith, a total of nearly 300 riflemen out of the total force of 1100. It was a march that was, according to Simpson, "...perhaps, the most arduous during the revolutionary war..." After departing from Fort Western (present-day Augusta, Maine) the force, with leaky and heavy bateaux, made its way up the Kennebec River, laboriously portaging the boats and supplies around the falls of Norridgewock and Skowhegan. While three men managed each bateau, Simpson invited Henry, "his messmate" aboard, and acting as steersman, with John Tidd and James Dougherty as boatmen, Simpson's vessel was "...able to lead any boat in the river." (Interestingly, Tidd was later with the rifle corps in Schoharie.) On October 23, while on the Dead River, the crew members found themselves on the opposite bank from the rest of the army, where all of the provisions, tents and camp equipage were. Here there was a falls of four feet and a substantial distance of raging white water.

Few would dare the passage, but there "...were two men, and only two who had skill and courage to dare it. Need lieutenant Simpson on an occasion like this; be named; he accompanied by John Tidd, entered his empty boat. What skill in boatmanship! What aptitude with the paddle was here exhibited." Displaying "his amazing skill," Simpson shot the falls, along with several soldiers who leaped aboard at the last moment. Simpson told the men in the bow to lay hold of some shrubbery, failing that, the boat turned about several times and those in the bow leaped ashore, kicking the craft out while doing so, and hitting the current broadside, it was rolled over, spilling Simpson and Henry into the raging foam. After surfacing, the pair attempted the "art of swimming...but it was a tipsy-turvy business" as "the force of the water threw me often heels-over-head." For several hundred yards the pair were swept, until, virtually resigned to their fate, they found themselves surfaced in an eddy, where they were hauled ashore, Simpson with his gold laced hat still on his head, and water pouring from their lungs.

When approaching the head of the Dead River and nearing the first of what are called "the chain of ponds," Simpson and his crew determined to out-pull the Virginia riflemen. These latter "had taken up the idea, that they were our superiors in every military qualification and ought to lead," but the Pennsylvanians soon overtook and out-paced their competitors, having however, an unfair advantage—Henry had been on an advance scout and already knew the passage from the first to the second pond.

Meanwhile, as supplies dwindled and the trek through the wilderness surpassed previously expected distances, the men began to suffer from hunger, disease and exposure to the harsh elements. Half of the force under Colonel Roger Enos deserted and returned to the settlements. Moccasins, soaps, candle wax and anything edible were consumed by the starving remnant. A number perished from various causes. On November 1, Simpson, leading the way, called a halt before a gloomy swamp some three-quarters of a mile wide and covered with a half-inch thickness of ice, and waited for the stragglers and maimed of Hendricks' and Smith's companies to come up. "Entering the pond, (Simpson foremost) and breaking the ice here and there with the butts of our guns and feet, as occasion required, we were soon waist deep in the mud and water." Shortly after passing "the Chaidiere lake," today's Lake Megantic, Simpson gave a dying fellow soldier half of his last pittance of food before leaving him. On another occasion when young Henry accidentally spilled the precious contents of another man's kettle, the latter sprung to his gun and threatened to shoot him. But the interference of Simpson, "...soon made us friends." The contents of the kettle were actually that of a dog, a pet of an officer. So acute were his sufferings and privations in the trackless wilderness Henry contemplated suicide, but "One principal cause of change...in my sentiments, was the jovial hilarity of my friend Simpson. At night, warming our bodies at an immense fire, our compatriots joined promiscuously around—to animate the company, he would sing 'Plato'; his sonorous voice gave spirit to my heart, and the moral of the song, consolation to my mind."

Finally, on November 3, when the men were on the verge of giving up hope, Arnold, who had heroically gone ahead to the French settlements, returned with cattle. On the evening of November 13, the troops, or rather the scarecrows calling themselves such, crossed the St. Lawrence River and began the siege—if it may be called that—of Quebec. On November 16, Lieutenant Simpson, in charge of 22 men of the company, led his men on the run to a ferry carrying cattle, with the shout of "come on lads!" The boatmen attempted to set off but "Simpson, with his usual good humor, urged the race. Overtaking the scow, which had run aground, the men immediately leaped into the water. A moment later a well placed cannon shot from the garrison took off the leg of a riflemen. Simpson, "Whose heart was tender and kind," called to the men who bore the wounded man away to a shout of triumph from the enemy.

It is noteworthy that during that time in the American army, officers and men like Simpson and Henry could be associates, even close friends, with little regard to rank or class distinction. During the siege, Lieutenant Simpson said to Private Henry, "Jack, let us have a shot at those fellows," and off they would go in their game to pick off sentries with their accurate long rifles. Sometimes Simpson commanded detachments of the guard close to the ramparts. In the fatal and unsuccessful attack on December 31, 1775, Simpson was not found among the attackers, most of whom were killed or taken during the desperate assault. This caused speculation among his fellow Pennsylvanians regarding his courage, but Henry proved it to be otherwise. Wrote Henry, "Simpson, one of the most spirited and active of officers—always alert—always on duty, was traduced and vilified for a want of courage because he was not taken prisoner at Quebec. This small canton (Paxton) was bursting with falsehoods propagated on the subject." Simpson had been ordered to the Isle of Orleans by Colonel Arnold on December 29, according to a document produced by Henry. Simpson took command there. One rifle officer caused consternation there by keeping "open house," in other words, selling liquor illicitly, and "...had a short, but a luxurious and merry reign over that charming spot. He was not with us at the attack of the city, but gaily danced his way to quarters." It was Simpson's duty to put a halt to such activities.[139]

Less is known of the "excellent patriot" Simpson's career after the Canadian campaign, as he had no friend to write about his daily experiences. In early 1777, Simpson was chosen as an officer in Captain James Parr's company of Morgan's riflemen, and no doubt shared the fortunes of the rifle corps during the bloody fighting in New Jersey, Pennsylvania, at Saratoga, as well as the encampment of 1777-1778 at Valley Forge and Radnor. As one of the officers in Schoharie, Simpson probably took part in the Unadilla-Onoquaga campaign of October 1778. When Parr was promoted to major, Simpson was superseded to command of the company. As captain of one of the rifle companies,

Simpson's name is frequently mentioned in the journals kept on the Sullivan-Clinton expedition while his activities and that of his company are detailed in the chapter on that campaign. It was his company that solemnly interred the remains of Lieutenant Boyd and Private Parker at the Genesee Castle, also known as Little Beard's town, on September 14, 1779.

Simpson was retired on January 17, 1781,[140] but according to Henry had risen to the rank of general at some point before 1812. He died in June 1813, at the age of 80.

Thomas Boyd (1756 - 1779)

Deserved or not, there can be no doubt that Thomas Boyd is the best remembered officer of the rifle corps stationed in upstate New York. He was born in 1756, and like many another rifleman, was of Irish descent. It is said that his mother was of true Spartan spirit, for she bade her three sons to fight and, if necessary, die for their country rather than dishonor it. Indeed, two of her boys would never return home.

Thomas was enlisted and became a sergeant in Captain Mathew Smith's company of Thompson's Rifle Battalion on June 25, 1775. This unit is believed to have contained many of the men who had made up the notorious "Paxton Boys."[141] Having made the march to Cambridge in record time, Smith's company took part in the siege of Boston, and was one of the three rifle companies chosen to lead the main body of Colonel Benedict Arnold's troops during the ill-fated march to Quebec. It was at this time that 16-year-old John Joseph Henry deserted his own company and joined Smith's to be in on the march. He was a friend of Boyd's, and in his book detailing the hardships and travail of that "Band of Heroes," he often made mention of Boyd.

From Newburyport, Massachusetts, the riflemen boarded vessels or transports which brought them up to Cobourn's shipyard (Pittston, Maine), and from there, by bateaux, up the Kennebec River to Fort Western (Augusta). Here Colonel Arnold ordered Lieutenant Archibald Steele of Smith's company to select his companions for an extensive scouting mission "...for the purpose of ascertaining and marking the paths, used by the Indians at the numerous carrying-places in the wilderness...and also, to ascertain the course of the river Chaudiere, which runs from the height of land, towards Quebec." Steele selected Jesse Wheeler, George Merchant, and James Clifton of Morgan's, and Robert Cunningham, John Tidd (later on duty in Schoharie), John M'Kondy, and Thomas Boyd of Smith's company. Two beautiful birchbark canoes, in which Henry took delight and left detailed descriptions of, were provided. Two local guides, familiar with such watercraft and who knew the river as high up as the "Great Carrying Place," were found in the persons of Jeremiah Getchel and John Horne. Setting forth in their "light barks," Steele's canoe with five men, the other containing seven along with their arms, baggage and provisions, they made from fifteen to twenty miles per day. On September 23, 1775, they reached the remains of Fort Halifax (where a wooden blockhouse still stands today), and shortly thereafter made the portage at Norridgewock and Skowhegan Falls, blazing these and all lesser carrying places. On September 27, the scout reached the "twelve-mile carrying-ing-place," the farthest distance the guides had ever ascended. On one occasion, Henry and Boyd had a footrace to their canoes; Boyd won, but stepping on some moss "sunk ten feet into as cold water...as was ever touched." A "laughable occurrence," at least to Henry. The party passed several ponds and entered the Dead River, sometimes adding to their feeble supply of food by angling for trout and chubs. Evidently Boyd was something of a fisherman. After "observing low ground on the other side of the river, and an uncommon coldness in the water, returned with a dozen trout in less than an hour. On another occasion, Boyd had less luck hunting. He attempted to bring down a bull moose when his rifle made "but a trifling report" because he "had neglected to clean his gun that day; it made long fire," the bullet barely reaching its target. Henry thought this particular moose had horns that seemed to stand eighteen feet in the air. On October 4, they party found the cabin of Natanis, the chief they had orders to kill or capture. Bursting in the door, they failed to catch their recently departed prey. Actually, Natanis had continually eyed the advancing scout, and later with some of his warriors, joined Arnold's forces. Natanis, or perhaps his brother, Sabbatis, even left a map of birchbark inserted into a split of a stake near the bank of the stream to aid the riflemen as they threaded their way through the unknown wilderness. After making several carries and reaching the "height of land," the men were able to discern the Chaudiere River. Having reached their goal, the men hurried to return to the army, sometimes making 40 to 50 miles a day. On the return one of the bark canoes was torn asunder by a half submerged branch, but was promptly repaired by the guide, Getchel. Before embarking, Boyd picked up the other canoe and slipped on the bank. The canoe hit the angle formed by the bank and the water, and the fragile craft broke in two. Again, Getchel came to the rescue; sewing the rip with roots and covering it with pitch,

using a patch of birchbark a foot wide reaching to the gun-
wales. This was sewn at the edges and pitched. For addi-
tional security, a greasy bag of pork was laid over it. Soon
after this, several moose were killed to add to their nearly
exhausted food supply; some of the excess meat being preserved by jerking. But from the lack of anything other than
meat in their diet, the men soon grew emaciated and weak.
Near the end, Boyd momentarily nearly lost faith in surviving; "here, my worthy friend Boyd, unable to proceed, sunk
down upon a log," and "...endeavoring to insure comfort
and courage into his manly mind—it was in vain."

On the following day, the advance of the army came into
sight, to the "extatic joy" of the scout. By this point the men
had "...wan and haggard faces, and meager bodies,
and...monstrous beards," after an absence of 26 days. Here
it was learned two men who had been left at one of the lakes
had deserted their post, carrying all the food they could before rejoining the army. Meanwhile, Steele, Getchel and
Wheeler had gone ahead to bring aid to Henry, Boyd, and
the others.

We can be assured that Boyd, as one of the riflemen, was
in the forefront of the assault on Quebec. He was among the
number captured. There are several references to him by
Henry during his nine-month imprisonment. Although defeated, sickly, and with their clothing in tattered remnants,
"...even now, an idea of escape and vengeance inflamed the

breasts of many…" Boyd and Henry (who found himself in
the sergeant's mess), had but one coarse, blue blanket or
"stroud" between them, but it was considered a real comfort.
At first imprisoned in the "reguliers," the non-coms were
transferred to the Dauphin jail. The hard campaign, the assault, and disease were taking their toll. In Smith's company,
Henry states that "Out of sixty-five, who came on Abraham's
Plains in November, we had scarcely more than thirty, left
with us in prison," but evidently there were others in the
hospital. Plans for a mass escape attempt were formulated,
and "Boyd and others of the most spirit became majors, captains, lieutenants, etc. That which cheered me much, was
that the council assigned me, a first lieutenancy under my
friend Boyd, whose rigor and courage were unquestionable."
A major part of the plan was to have Boyd lead about 25
men equipped with secretly made spears in an attack on the
guard opposite the jail, while other groups were assigned by
the escape council to make similar assaults. A small body was
reserved to support Boyd "particularly by way of setting fire
to the jail, the guardhouse, and the buildings in its
neighborhood" to distract the British while the prisoners ran
to one of the gates. If possible, the men would turn the cannon upon the city while the army outside the walls, by a pre-
arranged signal, would enter through the St. John's gate. If
all failed or the plan went awry, all were to shift for themselves and hope for the best. A door, which was padlocked
on the inside, was the proposed route, but a foot of ice prevented its opening. When two men, without authority, began
chipping away at the ice, the sentries heard the telltale
sounds and the plot was quickly revealed. Boyd, among others, were named as those in the plot and taken to the governor's council. They were put under oath, and "…boldly ad-
mitted and justified the attempt." Upon his return to the
jail, "…my dear Boyd shed the tears of excruciating anguish
in my bosom, deploring our adverse fate." The men were

put in irons, but many deftly had them off in minutes. By using knives notched as saws and cutting off the heads of the rivets, the men were able to slip in and out of their shackles, when, and if the guard visited. An outbreak of scurvy and "iarrhoes" made their appearance in April and May, and whittled down the number of survivors. Journals indicate wild rumors ran through the jail—Washington had been killed, the Continental Army wiped out, the prisoners might be exchanged, or even sent to a South Seas island. Finally, in August 1775, the prisoners boarded ships, sailed out of the St. Lawrence and around New England to New York harbor, and were released at Elizabethtown Point in New Jersey. The terms were liberal for the paroled—they could not take up arms until the first of the year.[142]

Boyd is recorded as having been promoted to first lieutenant of the 1st Pennsylvania on January 14, 1778.[143] No doubt, as one of the chosen marksmen drafted into detached duty with Colonel Morgan's Rifle Corps, Boyd shared the fortunes and hardships of that regiment in its bloody engagements in New Jersey, Pennsylvania and New York, and its encampments at Morristown, Middlebrook and Valley Forge. Arriving in the Schoharie Valley in the summer of 1778, Lieutenant Boyd, of Captain Parr's Company, probably saw service on numerous scouts, and was likely with his company on the Unadilla-Onoquaga raid in October. He wintered at the Middle Fort, and perhaps saw more service on scouts in the spring. When the rifle corps was preparing to pull out of Schoharie, on June 11, 1779, Cornelia Becker is said to have publicly accused Boyd of being the father of her unborn baby and called down the vengeance of heaven upon him.[144] Boyd is recorded as having led a number of scouts during the campaign against the Indians. General Clinton sent him out in charge of nine riflemen to inform General Sullivan that General Poor had met his forces and that they would meet at the appointed rendezvous location at Tioga.[145] Boyd fought at Newtown on August 29, and accompanied the rifle corps on its mission of destruction.

On September 13, General Sullivan gave verbal orders to Lieutenant Boyd to take 5 or 6 men and find Little Beard's Town (also called Genesee Castle), a substantial Seneca town located near the Genesee River. Instead, Boyd promptly broke this order by taking along, in addition, a number of volunteers, totaling some 28 men. This was Boyd's first mistake. Such a force could not accomplish any more than a half dozen could have and increased the chances of being discovered by the enemy. In this case, they were too small to adequately defend themselves. When Boyd, attempting to take a prisoner, allowed his men to fire on a party of Indians, the report of the shots, as well as the flight of the survivors could have disclosed his position to the enemy—a second error. Boyd's third blunder was when he permitted his men to pursue a small number of Indians, putting his force in a position to be ambushed. This series of blunders was to cost him dearly. Surrounded on all sides, the little party fought to the death. Only Boyd and Private Michael Parker were taken alive. A few thought Boyd had been wounded during the unequal, desperate combat. As American riflemen and light infantry rushed upon the scene, the enemy quickly departed with their prisoners. Interrogated by Colonel John Butler at Little Beard's Town on the west side of the Genesee, Boyd answered all questions. The question is whether he did so as a result of being tortured or after he was ruthlessly turned over to the Indians, or, if, after the departure of Butler and Brant, he was pounced upon by the Indians. Historians of the last century painted Boyd as a heroic martyr for America, overlooking the fact that, by disobeying orders, he unnecessarily led a number of brave men to their deaths. In fact, had he lived, one wonders if he would have been court-martialed rather than praised for his actions.

When the bodies of the two riflemen were found by the American army, Boyd's head was missing. It was found in one of the cabins. His scalp was still moist, stretched on a hoop, and painted—Captain Simpson recognized it by its "long brown and silky hair."[146] It was preserved in his memory. Thomas Campbell, of the 4th Pennsylvania told Henry, "I procured a needles and thread ...and sewed the corpse up as well as I could. As to the head of Michael Parker, it could not be found."[147] During the following year when some prisoners taken in Schoharie were in the Genesee Valley, the Indians told them that the head they were using as a sort of football was that of Boyd's. Perhaps, as Parker's head was reported missing, it was really his. Also, some prisoners taken from the Wyoming Valley that same year claimed that a warrior armed with a sword boasted it had belonged to Boyd—the Americans rose up one night on their captors and slew them, taking Boyd's purported sword with them.

Buried with the honors of war by Captain Simpson's company, their remains were not to be left in peace. Early curiosity seekers among the first settlers to the region exhumed some of the bodies of Boyd's men and took buttons, fragments of uniforms, etc., as souvenirs. In 1841 and 1842 the cherished remains of the fallen were gathered up, and with great fanfare, reinterred in the new Mount Hope Cemetery located in Rochester, New York at a site called "Revolutionary Hill," now known as "Rochester Hill."[148] However, severe flooding and erosion began to expose fragments of the remains and vandals began taking away bones of the slain soldiers. Again, the remains were reburied, this time on level ground. Around the turn of the century a monument was put up in their memory. Besides this monument, another may be seen at the ambush site near Groveland, and another at the site of the Genesee Castle. The latter is known as the Boyd-Parker Memorial and is located near Leicester. A great and ancient oak tree, still living, was remembered by early settlers, some of whom were veterans of the expedition, as the one Boyd and Parker were tied to (or near) and then tortured.

Monument to Lt. Boyd and Michael Parker on the site of their last battle near present Groveland, New York. Photo by author.

Physically, Boyd was a huge man, described as the "strongest and largest man among us" and "the strongest and stoutest man of the party, and perhaps of the army."[149]

Boyd's two brothers, William and John, also saw rigorous service with the Continental Army. William, a lieutenant, was killed on September 11, 1777, and John served in the army from 1776 until 1781, when he retired from the 3rd Pennsylvania. Made captain of a Bedford Country company of Rangers, he was captured by Indians in June of 1781, and taken to the Genesee Valley—the area where his brother had been tortured. He was confined in Canada on an island in the St. Lawrence, near Montreal, and exchanged in the spring of 1782.[150]

Gabriel Long

Made a captain of the 11th Virginia on July 23, 1776, Gabriel Long was said to have been Colonel Daniel Morgan's favorite captain. No doubt the fact that Long was a fellow Virginian was a factor. The 11th was designated the 7th Virginia on September 14, 1778, with Long's designation as such.

Undoubtedly, Long's career in the military was an active one as he shared in the campaigns and hardships of his regiment.

George Washington Park Custis, an adopted son of the general, had an interview with Morgan when he was serving in Congress during the years 1797 to 1799. An adventure involving Captain Long occurred, according to Custis, on the morning of the Battle of Monmouth on June 28, 1778. A detachment of Washington's famed Life-Guard and one from Morgan's riflemen under Long "made a brilliant dash at a party of the enemy which they surprised while washing at a brook that ran through an extensive meadow. Seventeen grenadiers were made prisoners, and borne off in the very face of the British light-infantry, who fired upon their daring assailants, and immediately commenced a hot pursuit; yet Long displayed such consummate ability as well as courage, that he brought off his party, prisoners and all, with only the loss of one sergeant wounded." Morgan, having listened with great anxiety to the heavy firing, awaited the detachment's return. "Charmed with the success of the enterprise, in the return of the troops almost unharmed, and in the prisoners taken, Morgan wrung the favorite captain by the hand, and paid his compliments to the officers and men of his own corps, and of the Life-Guard." Upon viewing the dirty and bespattered condition of the proud members who composed this detachment of the Life-Guard, Morgan, the "Leader of the Woodsmen" made the surrounding countryside reverberate with his well known "stentorian laugh." This daring raid is documented in a letter from Morgan to Washington, but is dated June 17.[151]

Custis, in his recollections of his interview with Morgan, related another exciting incident involving Captain Long. At some point during the war, thought to be in New Jersey possibly around the time of the Monmouth battle, General Washington, in need of intelligence regarding the positions of the enemy, summoned Colonel Morgan to headquarters. Morgan was instructed to take a party of men and reconnoiter the enemy lines, but by no means bring on a skirmish with the foe as "...no force of circumstance will excuse the discharge of a single rifle on you part." Calling on Captain Long, Morgan ordered him to select a sergeant and 20 riflemen for the daring enterprise. Just after midnight, with the going down of the moon, Long cried, "up sergeant, stir up your men!" and twenty "athletic figures," in an instant, were upon their feet, and marched away in Indian file with the "quick, yet light and stealthy step of the woodsman." Just before dawn, having successfully completed the object of the mission without any discovery, the detachment prepared to return to camp. At a little eminence Morgan called a halt to allow his men a little rest before resuming their trek when a body of horse troops was spied coming along the road leading directly to the riflemen. "Down, boys, down," Morgan called to his men, as each scattered behind cover, the spot perfect for an ambuscade. Morgan looked at Long and Long looked at Morgan while the riflemen, with panting chests and sparkling eyes, awaited some signal from their officers "to let the ruin fly." Unable to resist the thought of pulling off the perfect ambuscade, Morgan "Forgetful of consequences, reckless of everything but his enemy now within his grasp, he waved his hand," and was greeted with the shattering blast of his men's unerring rifles. "At point-blank distance, the certain and deadly aim of the Hunting Shirts of the Revolutionary army is too well-known to history to need remark at this time of day. In the instance we have to record, the effects of the fire of the riflemen were tremendous. Of the horsemen, some had fallen to rise no more, while their liberated chargers rushed wildly over the adjoining plains; others, wounded, but entangled with their stirrups, were dragged by the furious animals expiringly along, while the very few who were unscathed spurred hard to regain the shelter of the British lines." As "the picturesque forms of the woodsmen appeared among the foliage," reloading their pieces, the gigantic stature of Morgan, as though in deep thought, stood apart. He gave no orders to his men to follow up on their little victory, or to remove from their victims the clothing and equipment always sorely needed by their own forces. A conch shell* "from which he had blown full many a note of battle and of triumph on the fields of Saratoga hung idly by his side," as Morgan turned to his captain and exclaimed, "Long, to the camp, march." With their rifles at the trail (carried level at their sides), the men, mystified by their commander's behavior, they made their way back to camp. Morgan, having disobeyed the explicit orders of his beloved Washington, was sure his illustrious military career was at an end. At first ordered to his quarters, Morgan was infinitely relieved when he was invited, with all of the other high-

---

* According to Custis, "Morgan was in a habit of using a conch-shell frequently during the heat of the battle, with which he would blow a loud and warlike blast. This he said was to inform his boys that he was still alive, and from many parts of the field was beholding their prowess; and, like the last signal of a celebrated sea-warrior of another hemisphere, was expecting that 'every many would do his duty.'" Interestingly, David Ellerson, of Long's company, claimed that, while serving as a Ranger in Schoharie, the leader of a scout also used a conch shell to assemble the men should they become separated. A conch shell, said to have been used by the settlers of Harrodsburg, Kentucky, is still in existence.

ranking officers, to dine with Washington during which the commander-in-chief proposed a toast to his health, removing all apprehensions of the famed fire officers.[152]

During the rifle corps' sojourn in Schoharie, in which Long commanded one of the two companies, he won an early success in the ambush and defeat of Captain Charles Smith and his band of Loyalists in early August, 1778. One of the letters to Governor Clinton stated, "Capt. Long of the Riffle men fired at and shot Smith through the head," and another that he "fell in with them, Kill'd Smith & Brought in his Scalp."[153]

Long resigned his commission on May 13, 1779, the command of his company going to Captain-Lieutenant Philip Slaughter. Lt. Elijah Evans commanded some of Long's men on the expedition against the Onondagas in April, 1779. His date of birth is unknown. The intrepid Captain Long died on February 3, 1827.**

William Stevens

Except for several entries in Lt. Col. William Butler's journal, and Jeptha Simms' brief account of his death, we have scant information on William Stevens. We do know that he was a member of Captain Parr's Company, indicating he was from Pennsylvania.[154] As a member of the rifle corps, he was, no doubt, a veteran of many hard fought battles and campaigns.

Lieutenant Stevens seems to have been an active, dependable officer, according to Butler's journal of the expedition that destroyed Onoquaga and Unadilla in 1778. On

---

** According to *Historical Register of Virginia in the Revolution*, by John H. Gwethney, Richmond, 1938, Long was awarded 4000 acres for his wartime services.

October 1, Stevens, entrusted with 29 men from both the rifle corps and the local militia, was sent to the fringes of the Schoharie Valley to watch all roads and passages and prevent intelligence of the proposed expedition of the enemy. Later, Stevens and Lieutenant Reuben Long took out scouts and returned with a prisoner. Also, Butler credited a scout under Stevens' command as having captured a Loyalist by the name of Glasford, who was later put to use as a guide. On the evening of October 7, Butler again sent out Stevens to "...advance and reconnoiter the country about Anaquage." As ordered, the lieutenant returned the following day and gave Butler "...as good a description of the settlement as he was able to discover from the adjacent mountains." Thus did Lieutenant Stevens play a major role in this successful operation.[155]

Evidently Stevens' enlistment period either expired in late 1779 or early 1780, as many others of the rifle corps did, or he resigned his commission, as we find him back in the Schoharie Valley where he enlisted as a private in the local militia. What prompted Stevens to give up his rank in the Continental Army and enlist in the militia is unknown. But like several of the nine other riflemen who returned to the area at about this time, a woman is a likely possibility. However, if this is true, a look at local church records reveals no marriage.

We catch one final glimpse of a Stevens in April of 1780, almost certainly William. On April 2, a scout of 14 men under Lieutenant Alexander Harper was sent out from the Schoharie forts by Colonel Peter Vroman (Vrooman) into the Harpersfield area, near the headwaters of the Delaware River, to watch the conduct of certain "suspected" persons, and if possible to make a quantity of maple sugar. A heavy snow had fallen and, not expecting an attack, the party began their manufacture of sugar when they were surprised by an enemy force. According to Simms it consisted of 43 Indians and 7 Loyalists under the command of Joseph Brant. The date was April 7. So complete was Brant's approach that not a gun was fired at the enemy. Two Americans were shot down and eleven more captured. According to Simms, "Poor Stevens, who was on that day sick in bed and unable to proceed with the prisoners, was killed and scalped in cold blood." Thus was Stevens killed in the first blow of vengeance conducted by the enemy in return for the destruction wreaked upon them by Sullivan's army. Stevens had been a part of that expedition the previous year.

Brant's force had been on their way to the Schoharie settlements to lay waste that area when they happened on Harper's scout. Lieutenant Harper, by falsely admitting to Brant that a force of 300 Continental troops had just arrived at the forts, dissuaded the Mohawk chieftain from going there, helping to save Schoharie from a devastating raid. The prisoners were taken to Fort Niagara, which, no doubt, was the destination of Stevens' scalp.[156] It is unfortunate that so little is known of this man. Even Heitman's register of Continental officers has no reference to Stevens after 1780.

Elijah Evans

Elijah Evans, a Marylander, was ensign of Stephenson's Maryland and Virginia Rifle Regiment as of May, 1776; promoted to lieutenant, August 10, 1776. Taken prisoner at Fort Washington, November 16, 1776, he survived a terrible ordeal as a captive.

During the Battle of Fort Washington, on Manhattan, some 400 riflemen under Colonel Moses Rawling were entrenched outside the fort and threw back several assaults of crack German troops. Only when the rifles began to foul up, did they retire to the main works. Soon after, because it was considered untenable, they surrendered. Of the 450 casualties inflicted upon the Germans, most were from the rifles of the sharpshooters or the artillery. Most of the 2,800 Americans captured were to die horrendous deaths in British prison ships.[157] Evans was among the few to survive. Back in the Continental Army, and according to Heitman, he was promoted to captain of Rawling's Continental Regiment on April 10, 1778.[158] Stationed in Schoharie at the Middle Fort, he commanded a detachment of riflemen on the Van Schaik expedition against the Onondagas, in which he is mentioned as a lieutenant. On the march to the Onondaga towns, his men served as flankers; on the return they formed the advance and quickly beat off an Indian attack over Onondaga Creek (present-day Syracuse).

Evans retired from the service on January 1, 1781, and died in 1801.

Reuben Long

Reuben Long became sergeant of the 11th Virginia, September 26, 1776; ensign December 16, 1776; second lieutenant, June 1, 1777; regiment designated 7th Virginia, September 14, 1778; first lieutenant, May 10, 1779; transferred to 3rd Virginia, February 12, 1781, and served until close of the war.[159]

Long served on the Unadilla-Onoquaga expedition in October, 1778, and is mentioned several times in Colonel William Butler's Journal. He was awarded 2,666 acres for his services in the war.

Philip Slaughter

A Virginian, Philip Slaughter became a second lieutenant of the 11th Virginia on July 23, 1776: first lieutenant, March 14,

1777; regimental paymaster, March 14, 1777; regiment designated the 7th Virginia, September 14, 1778; promoted to captain-lieutenant, November 1, 1778; to captain (upon the resignation of Captain Gabriel Long) May 13, 1779; and retired on February 12, 1781.[160]

Slaughter commanded one of the two rifle companies during the Sullivan-Clinton campaign of June-October, 1779. He was awarded 5,000 acres for his services in the war, and settled in the Culpeper, Virginia region.

Henry Henly

Henly served as quartermaster for the rifle corps until promoted to ensign of the 4th Pennsylvania, on July 2, 1779; to lieutenant on April 17, 1780; transferred to 2d Pennsylvania, January 1, 1783 and served to June 3, 1783.[161]

John Coleman

Coleman was an ensign in the 2d Virginia, from July 4 to December, 1779. He also served as adjutant for the rifle corps until August 1, 1779. After the war he was awarded 2,666 acres for his services.[162]

Benjamin Ashby

Ensign of the 11th Virginia, from Nov. 30, 1776; Regimental Quartermaster, Jan. 1, 1777; 2d lieutenant, June 1, 1777; regiment designated 7th Virginia, September 14, 1778; 1st lieutenant, March 13, 1779 (also served as paymaster; transferred to 3rd Virginia, Jan. 1, 1781; retired Jan. 1, 1783.)[163]

Daniel Shute

Aide-de-Camp to General Lincoln, October 27, 1777 to January, 1778; Surgeon's Mate Hospital Department, July 16, 1778 to June 16, 1779; Surgeon 4th Massachusetts, April 11, 1782 to June, 1783. Shute was attached to the rifle corps as a surgeon until he left on June 15, 1779, and was one of the few men not drafted from Pennsylvania, Virginia, or Maryland. He died on April 18, 1829.[164]

Benjamin Chambers

Enlisted as a private in Thompson's Pennsylvania Rifle Battalion, June 27, 1775; 2d lieutenant, 1st Continental Infantry, January 5, 1776; discharged on August, 1776; Ensign 1st Pennsylvania, June 2, 1778; lieutenant, September 13, 1779; resigned November 26, 1780. He died on December 29, 1813.[165]

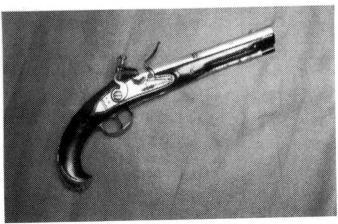

An American made pistol with a rifled barrel, typical of an officer's sidearm. Courtesy of the H. Kels Swan Collection of the American Revolution. Photo by Gilbert Dabkowski.

Part Three

The Riflemen Who Returned To Schoharie 1779 - 1783

"This country has been made by Timothy Murphys, the men in the ranks. Conditions here called for the qualities of heart and head that Tim Murphy had in such abundance. Our histories should tell us more of the men in the ranks, for it was to them, more than to the generals, that we were indebted for our military victories."

Gov. Franklin Delano Roosevelt
(President of the United States from 1932 to 1945)

In the summer of 1778, six of the eight companies of the specially raised rifle corps under Colonel Daniel Morgan were disbanded, the men returning to their original regiments. Only the companies of Captains Parr and Long remained. These were detached to the Schoharie frontier where they further distinguished themselves in operations in that area, as well as during the offensive campaigns against Unadilla and Onoquaga (October, 1778); with Van Schaik at Onondaga (April, 1779); and Sullivan's Indian Campaign (June-October, 1779). In November 1779, these last two companies were broken up at West Point, upon Washington's orders. Some of the men had signed on for the war and went back to their original units as musketmen. Others had enlisted for three years, which were expiring at about this time. Among these were ten riflemen who returned to Schoharie. They were among the best members of the rifle corps, and became well-known folk heroes in the area.

The riflemen who joined the Schoharie militia units were Lt. William Stevens who was killed on April 7, 1780 (see his biography among those of the officers); William Lloyd, Timothy Murphy, David Ellerson (wounded on June 27, 1779), Joseph Evans, Zachariah Tufts (wounded October 17, 1780), William Leek, John Wilbur, Philip Hoever and Felix Hoever. Often led by the already well-known Murphy, most of the men continually enlisted in the same units together, a strong indication of their close friendship. Records would indicate that women were a primary reason for their return. Seven of the riflemen enlisted in Captain Bogart's Company of Colonel Harper's Regiment on May 1, 1780. When that enlistment expired, they enlisted in Captain Hager's Company of the 15th Regiment of Albany County, under the command of Colonel Peter Vroman (Vrooman) on Nov. 1, 1780. Ellerson lived to a ripe old age, and was interviewed by

Jeptha Simms, author of *The Frontiersmen of New York,* in 1837. Ellerson explained their duties as rangers to Simms:

> *The Ranger Service. – Most of the riflemen who continued in Schoharie during the war, and some of the more fearless citizens enlisted to perform the duty of scouts, more or less of whom, were constantly out from the Schoharie forts, in the summer season. They were called, there as elsewhere, "Rangers," a term very applicable. Their duties were at times of the most dangerous and fatiguing kind, and not unfrequently, in the fall and spring of the year, when they had to encamp on the ground at night without a fire, they suffered almost incredible hardships. The music of those scouts, was that produced by a conch-shell, which was carried by the leader, and served to call the party together when they chanced to become separated in the woods.[166]*

An earlier account had noted that a similar group of riflemen, when on their way to Boston in 1775, "...want nothing to preserve their health and courage but water from the spring, with a little parched corn, with what they can easily procure in hunting; and who, wrapped in their blankets, in the damp of night, would choose the shadow of a tree for their covering, and the earth for their bed."[167] When detached on scouts, besides their parched corn, a number of other foods that needed no cooking could be brought along including jerky, corn-meal, bread, cheese, dried fruits, nuts, perhaps smoked fish, and a canteen of rum, cider, flip, or "kill-devil." Flip was a mixture of rum and cider. What was known affectionately as "kill-devil" was a mixture of cider and liquor, often with sugar, butter, or cinnamon added, and whenever possible, heated with a red hot poker. While rolled up in their blanket on damp ground in some cheerless part of the dark forest, the ranger went to sleep never completely sure of awakening.

Against these riflemen of Schoharie, were extremely formidable opponents—a number of Butler's Rangers and most of the warriors of the Six Nations. Active, incredibly effective partisans, the Loyalist Rangers and their Iroquois allies were both hated and feared for their successes as well as their outrages, and their ability to strike and terrorize virtually anywhere, at nearly anytime, on the New York and Pennsylvania frontiers. Morgan's riflemen were among their few equals in forest fighting—at least until the latter part of the war when able frontier leaders like Willett could muster up enough courage in the militia to stand them off.

The riflemen who served in Schoharie—wild, free-spirited, and rollicking individuals, contrasted strongly with the majority of the settlers, who were hard-working, family oriented, church going folk of Dutch and German origin. Indeed, muster rolls indicate that, after the departure of the Loyalists (often Scottish or English), a whopping 97% of the local militiamen of the valley were Dutch or German. While many of these people felt little desire to support either side in the beginning of hostilities, the British policy of encouraging and supporting raids on the frontier inhabitants had the effect of necessarily pushing most of these people into the rebel camp. A steadfast loyalty to their homes and farms helped them withstand astounding losses in life and property (virtually every home in the valley was destroyed by the end of the hostilities). Their bullish stubbornness not only saved their own land but also prevented the caving in of the frontier, "the back door of the Revolution."

Numerous legends grew over the years concerning the exploits of the riflemen—most of which we can never be sure at this date, of the fraction of truth behind them. We do know that they performed heroically during the attack on the Middle Fort, when Murphy, Ellerson and others present, were, apparently, largely responsible for saving the fort. Some fought commendably with Captain Hager at Bouck's Island and Lake Utsayantha in November, 1781, and no doubt, someone or another, was almost constantly out on scout at any given time.

Riflemen and their weapons never failed to attract attention:

"The Indians make use of rifled guns for the most part, and there is such a difference between these sort of Guns and Smooth bored, that if I was in an Engagement with the Savages, I would rather Stand my chance with one of the former Sort, which might require a minute to clean, load and discharge, than be possessed with a Smooth bored gun which I could discharge three times in ye same space, for at 150 yards distance, with the one, I can put a ball within a foot or Six Inches of ye mark, whereas with the other, I can Seldom or ever hit the board of two feet wide & Six feet long."

Edward Shippen, 1756
(Pennsylvania Archives, First Series, vol.2, pp 642-643)

"Yesterday the company was supplied with a small quantity of powder from the magazine, which wanted airing, and was not in good order for rifles; in the evening, however, they were drawn out to show the gentlemen of the Town their dexterity at shooting. A clapboard, with a mark the size of a dollar, was put up; they began to fire offhand, and the bystanders were surprised, few shots being made that were not close to or in the paper. When they had shot for a time in this way, some lay on their back, some on their breast or side, others ran twenty or thirty steps, and firing appeared to be equally certain of the mark. With this performance the company was more than satisfied, when a young man took up the board in his hand, not by the end, but by the side, and holding it as it was held before, the second brother shot as the former had done. By this exercise I was more astonished than pleased. But will you believe me when I tell you, that one of the men took the board, and placing it between his legs, stood with his back to the tree while another drove the center. What would a regular army of considerable strength in the forests of America do with one thousand of these men, who want nothing to preserve their health and courage but water from the spring, with a little parched corn, with what they can easily procure in hunting; and who, wrapped in their blankets, in the damp of night, would choose the shade of a tree for their covering, and the earth for their bed?"

Extract of a Letter to a Gentleman in Philadelphia, Describing a Shooting Match Held by Captain Michael Cresap's Company of Riflemen, 1775.

"Several different kinds of articles are manufactured at Lancaster by German mechanics, individually, principally for the people of the town and the neighbourhood. Rifled barrel guns however are to be excepted, which, although not as handsome as those imported from England, are more esteemed by the hunters, and are sent to every part of the country.

"The rifled barrel guns, commonly used in America, are nearly of the length of a musket, and carry leaden balls from the size of thirty to sixty in the pound (from .53 to .42 caliber). Some hunters prefer those of a small bore, because they require but little ammunition; others prefer such as have a wide bore, because the wound which they inflict is more certainly attended with death; the wound, however, made by a ball discharged from one of these guns, is always very dangerous. The inside of the barrel is fluted, and the grooves run in a spiral direction from one end of the barrel to the other, consequently when the ball comes out it has a whirling motion round its own axis, at the same time that it moves forward, and when it enters into the body of an animal, it tears up the flesh in a dreadful manner. The best of powder is chosen for the rifled barrel gun, and after a proper portion of it is put down the barrel, the ball is inclosed [sic] in a small bit of linen rag, well greased at the outside, and then forced down with a thick ramrod. The grease and the bits of rag, which are called patches, are carried in a little box at the but-end [sic] of the gun. The best rifles are furnished with two triggers, one of which being first pulled sets the other, that is, alters the spring so that it will yield even to the slight touch of a feather. They are also furnished with double sights along the barrel, as fine as those of a surveying instrument. An experienced marksman, with one of these guns, will hit an object not larger that a crown piece, to a certainty, at the distance of one hundred yards. Two men belonging to the Virginia rifle regiment, a large division of which was quartered in this down [sic] during the war, had such a dependence on each other's dexterity, that the one would hold a piece of board, not more than nine inches square, between his knees, whilst the other shot at it with a ball at the distance of one hundred paces. This they used to do alternately, for the amusement of the town's people, as often as they were called upon. Numbers of people in

Lancaster can vouch for the truth of this fact. Were I, however, to tell you all the stories I have heard of the performance of riflemen, you would think the people were most abominably addicted to lying. A rifle gun will not carry shot, nor will it carry a ball much farther than one hundred yards with certainty."

Isaac Weld
Travels Though The States of North America, 1799

William Leek (1747 ? - after 1820)

What we know of William Leek comes largely from Simms' *Frontiersmen of New York* and his pension papers. Born in 1747, Leek joined Captain John Lowdon's Company of Thompson's Rifle Battalion at Sunbury, Pennsylvania, along with a number of other noted frontiersmen, including Tim Murphy, in June 1770. In fact, Murphy and Leek seemed to have been closely connected throughout much of the war, often serving in the same companies, forging similar war records for themselves.

Thompson's riflemen marched to Cambridge, outside of Boston, in record time, tarring and feathering Loyalists along the way, putting on shooting demonstrations to amaze the New Englanders, harassing the British and when idle, harassing each other. Leek claimed to have been present at the Battle of Long Island (August 27, 1776), and with Colonel Hand's riflemen involved in the skirmishing on Long Island and the battles around New York City. At this time he was a member of Captain Parr's Company.

In early 1777, Leek was drafted into Morgan's Rifle Battalion, where he probably saw action in New Jersey and at Saratoga. Thompson's Rifle Battalion, commanded by Colonel Edward Hand, was designated the "First Regiment" of the Continental Line. Captain James Parr and 50 men were transferred, on detached duty, to Colonel Daniel Morgan's command for the unit. On paper, each man kept his original unit designation. Among the 50 were Murphy and Leek. On one occasion, in early July 1778, Murphy, David Ellerson and Zachariah Tufts volunteered to go ahead of the advancing riflemen and reconnoiter the retreating British as they departed from Raritan Bay in New Jersey. It was here that Ellerson claimed to have captured Sir Henry Clinton's private coach. After this, Captains Parr and Long were detached to the Schoharie, New York area along with Lt. Col. William Butler's 4th Pennsylvania. Here, besides going on scouts, Leek stated that he participated in three short Indian campaigns. Almost certainly these were Captain Long's victory over the Loyalists and the killing of Christopher Service in August 1778; the destruction of Unadilla and Onoquaga in October; and the Van Schaik expedition against the Onondaga towns in April 1779. All of these were noted successes and after a period of great frustrations for the local militias, were among the first offensive operations against the enemy on the New York frontier.

Leek's name does not appear on a muster role taken after the start of the Indian expedition under Sullivan and Clinton in 1779, so he might have been among the detachment ordered to remain at the Middle Fort in Schoharie. He acted as a "ranger," as did most of the other nine riflemen who returned to the area. On May 1, 1780, he enlisted in Captain Bogart's Company of Colonel Harper's Regiment as a private, serving until November 1 of that year. Leek's name is encountered several times in Simms' history. He seems to have been involved in a number of exciting episodes and exploits at about this time.

On about the 25th of July, 1780, William Bouck, an elderly man, a girl named Nancy Lattimore, and a female slave and her three children were captured by Seth's Henry, the notorious Schoharie chieftain, and three other Indians, about two miles from the Upper Fort. A scout of four militiamen, including Bouck's son, was fired upon by these Indians when out near Harpersfield. One of the scouts was wounded. The next morning, when it became evident that Bouck was missing, Captain Jacob Hager ordered out about 20 men under the command of Lieutenants Ephraim Vrooman and Joseph Harper, to pursue the captors, conjecturing the enemy would take the usual route towards Harpersfield. They came upon a trail left by a slave boy named Derek, who left an impression of his heel in the path when he could do so without being seen by his captors. The first scouting detachment fortunately fell in with the pursuing party, and proceeding on, arrived at the place of the shooting. Discovering the trail of the enemy, they began to ascend a nearby summit. Three of the Indians, feeling themselves secure, were casually mending their moccasins, while Seth's Henry had ascended to the top of the summit to keep an eye out for pursuers. From his elevated position, the Indian completely overlooked his approaching foes, and returned to his party. He told them they were out of danger just as the Americans gained a view of them within rifle-shot distance. With some of the prisoners in the field of fire, the rescuers were prevented from instantly discharging a volley of balls, except for Leek, who, having a fair aim upon an Indian, "snapped and his rifle unfortunately missed fire." The Indians, instantly "sprang to their feet, seized their weapons, and leaving their prisoners and packs, giving a whoop and exclaiming 'Yankees,' fled barefooted down the mountain." If Leek's rifle had not failed him at this critical moment, he, rather than his friend Murphy who later is said to have received the credit, might have gone down in history as the slayer of Seth's Henry. Nonetheless, the object of the operation, the rescue of the prisoners, was entirely successful.[168]

Leek evidently was something of a humorous sort, judging from an anecdote related by Simms. On August 9, not long after the successful rescue, a scout consisting of Leek, one of the Hoevers (either Philip or Felix, both riflemen), and Conradt Winnie, a local ranger, was sent out from the Upper Fort by Captain Hager. The men were ordered not to fire if the enemy was seen, but rather to return to communicate such information. After having proceeded some distance, the men sat down to eat their breakfasts, when a white man, painted as an Indian, emerged near a stream about 50 yards away. As he stooped to defecate, the easy mark became too tempting for Leek to resist. Being "a dead shot," he leveled his piece, fired and dropped the Loyalist (later believed to be a doctor, as medical instruments were found about his person). Immediately the woods became alive with green coats and painted flesh as a horde of about 80 Indians and Tories hotly pursued our heroes. Hoever and Winnie fled one way while Leek ran another. Evidently Leek was chased up, on, and over Panther Mountain, splashed across the Schoharie River, broke into the clearing around the Upper Fort, and after a race of nine or ten miles, finally gained entrance to the fort, with the Indians hot on his heels. In fact, so close were they, that an alarm could not be given, and a number of the inhabitants, including women and children, were killed or carried off as a result. The graves of the slain may still be seen near the site of the fort. Undoubtedly, Leek was extremely athletic to have outrun the Indians; warriors, it has been said, that could run eighty miles between sunrise and sunset.[169]

On or around October 3, 1780, shortly after the marriage of Leek's friend, Tim Murphy to Margaret Feeck, a scout consisting of both of those riflemen as well as Robert Hutt and William Lloyd, the latter in command, was detached from the Middle Fort. The men covered much of the immense area to the west and south of the valley, and though they saw little sign of the Indians, captured a Loyalist near present-day Prattsville before slipping back into the fort on October 16.[170]

The next morning, Sir John Johnson, ravaging the Scho-harie Valley with a large force of the enemy, approached the Middle Fort. There a detachment of volunteers consisting of Leek, Murphy, Ellerson, one of the Hoevers, Wilbur, Tufts, Lloyd and seven local rangers encountered the 1,000 man force of Indians, Loyalists, British and Germans. They fought a delaying action so close and hot some of the men's hunting frocks were later discovered to have bullet holes. Leek also participated in the defense of the fort, firing through loopholes in the stockade at the enemy. He went out on several sorties, and rallied to Murphy and Ellerson's side when they refused, with their rifles, to allow a Continental officer to discuss surrender terms with the enemy.

Leek also served as a private in Captain Hager's Company, in Col. Vrooman's 15th Regiment of Albany County, and along with others was almost certainly continually out on scouts.

Sometime during the war, Leek began having an affair with Maria Becker, who was married to a Loyalist who fled to Canada. Maria became pregnant and according to records they were married in the summer of 1782, the birth of their child being shortly thereafter. After the war, Becker came back to regain his wife, but failed. Unfortunately nothing more is recorded. It would be interesting to know just what persuaded Becker to give up and return to Canada and what role Leek played in it. Also there seems to be no record of a divorce between Maria and Becker, a fact that was evidently overlooked in her marriage to William.[171]

In the spring of 1782, Murphy, who had spent the winter hunting in the nearby mountains, had dressed a number of deerskins. Deciding to break the monotony of camp life, he participated in a shoot at the Upper Fort. At 100 yards a large white oak tree was blazed. In the center of the circle a white piece of paper was attached with a brass nail. The riflemen lay at full length upon the ground, said in to be their favorite position, according to contemporary accounts, and rested their rifles upon their hats. All, including Leek, made close shots, but the legendary Murphy settled it by actually driving the nail in!

In the fall of 1799, William, evidently still living in the area, joined Murphy, Ellerson and another person not identified, for a shooting match at the residence of Captain Hager near Blenheim. The target, a piece of paper pinned on a board two feet long, was held between the knees of each man as the others took turns placing shots at 100 paces. The first three shots cut the paper—Murphy's drove the pin through the board.[172] The author has come across a number of contemporary descriptions of riflemen in various parts of the country holding shooting competitions in precisely this fashion.

At some point in time the Leeks moved further west and settled in Cayuga County in the vicinity of Locke, New York as one of the pioneer setters in that area. In 1820, at the age of 73, he received his pension. Being illiterate, he signed it with his "X" mark. The deposition also discloses he was a farmer and the worth of his ownings was $48.50.[173] Leek's name has not been discovered among the lists of Revolutionary War veterans buried in Cayuga County, indicating he might have moved elsewhere before his death.

A modern-day rifleman draws a bead on a board held between the knees of a trusting comrade. Photo by the author.

Zachariah Tufts (1757 ? - After 1818)

Of the ten known riflemen who returned to Schoharie, Zachariah Tufts is especially interesting as he is the only one who originated from New England rather than Pennsylvania or Virginia. Born in 1756, Tufts was from Keene County, New Hampshire, evidently raised on the frontier of the southwestern portion of that colony near the Vermont border. Most our knowledge of this Yankee rifleman comes from Simms' *Frontiersmen of New York* and Tufts' own pension papers.

In 1775, Tufts served for eight months as a private in Captain John Wood's Company of a Colonel Gerroshi's Regiment of the Massachusetts line. Possibly he fought at the

Battle of Bunker Hill on June 17, 1775, as he states in his pension deposition to have been stationed there. On January 1, 1776, he enlisted as a private in Captain Hale's Company under Colonel John Stark, a New Hampshire regiment, at Medford, Massachusetts. On January 1, 1777, he was drafted into Colonel Daniel Morgan's regiment of picked riflemen, serving for the next three years as a private until discharged at Schoharie on January 1, 1780.[174]

As one of Morgan's partisans, Tufts fought through the Jerseys, at Freeman's Farm, Bemis Heights, the Monmouth campaign, and Sullivan's Indian expedition.

A member of Captain Parr's Company, he volunteered to go ahead of the American army as the British forces retreated across New Jersey after the Battle of Monmouth (June 28, 1778), along with Tim Murphy, David Ellerson, and John Wilbur. This was the time Ellerson allegedly captured Sir Henry Clinton's coach.

After this, the companies of Captains Parr and Long, under Major Posey, were detached to the Schoharie frontier, arriving at the Middle Fort in late July and early August 1778. Tufts may have participated in the destruction of Unadilla and Onoquaga in October 1778, and was often employed on various scouts. One historian places him with Murphy and Ellerson when they captured the Loyalist Christopher Service, even shooting him at the same moment

Murphy did during an escape attempt, but it is not vouched for in any other account.[175] He was present on Sullivan's punitive expedition against the Iroquois and their Loyalist allies and his name is mentioned in conjunction with a story concerning Timothy Murphy. According to the legend, Tufts, Murphy, Joachim Folluck (the famed half-blood ranger), and Joseph Evans obtained leave to go out on a scout along the Chemung River where they espied three Indians towing a canoe up the rapids. One of the Indians was standing in the canoe steering it. No sooner had they spotted the enemy than Murphy said to his companions, "I've a notion to try the one standing in the canoe," but the distance being so great none believed there was much chance of hitting him. Nonetheless, Murphy fired and had his man, the latter falling into the river. On the way back to the encampment, a boy of about fifteen or sixteen years of age, who, upon sight of the riflemen, attempted to flee, was easily overtaken and bound. That night, the boy managed to escape, taking Murphy's rifle and moccasins with him. Stealing a rifleman's most cherished possession was in itself a dangerous undertaking, but it being Murphy's, doubly so. When he returned to camp Murphy received permission to go in search of his rifle. Returning to the area where the boy had first been encountered, they again discovered him driving cattle and followed him to a hut in the wilderness, into which they entered and retook the boy and found the rifle. Murphy, enraged, wanted to kill the boy. Ellerson and the others prevented him from doing so by asking him what he would have done had the situation been reversed and it was he who was a prisoner. Murphy, calming down, relented, and then understood. The lad and another prisoner, lately taken, were brought back to camp.[176] Tufts, as a member of Captain Simpson's company, continued on the campaign and fought at Newtown on August 27, 1779.

After the return of the troops from the expedition, Tufts returned to Schoharie, where he may have married at this time. His wife, Mary, was eight years his junior. He was employed as a ranger and was often detached on scouts. He enlisted in May 1780, in Captain Isaac Bogart's Company of Colonel Harper's regiment and served until November 1, 1780, when he was discharged. After this he served at various times with Captain Jacob Hager's Company, 15th Regiment of Albany County.

On October 17, 1780, a force of about 1,000 British, Loyalists, Indians and Germans under Colonel John Johnson entered and began the sacking of the Schoharie Valley. A scouting party was sent out from the Middle Fort under Major Thomas Eckerson, of which Tufts and several of his fellow riflemen were members. They soon fell in with an advance party of Indians. After several minutes of close action, the rangers were ordered back to the fort. The entire enemy force now pursued the scouts and several received bullet holes through their frocks. (Incidentally, they also wore neckerchiefs around their heads that day as it was windy). After Murphy's famous mutiny when the commandant attempted to parley with the enemy (both Murphy and Ellerson had extra prices on their scalps, or so the latter claimed), a party of Indians was seen approaching the barn of John Becker. A small force from the fort was sent to stop them. However, they were forced to retire. As they entered the fort, Samuel Reynolds was shot through the head and Tufts received a ball in his arm.[177]

The enemy force soon proceeded up the valley, burning all they encountered. At the Lower Fort, sharpshooters were stationed in the tower of the church around which the fort was built. This church, bearing the scars of war, still stands and is the museum known today as the "Old Stone Fort."

Undoubtedly, Tufts went out on many scouts, always in danger, perhaps having untold adventures or hairbreadth escapes. His name is mentioned several times in conjunction with the many legendary exploits of his friend Timothy Murphy. One of these tales is said to have taken place shortly after Sir John Johnson passed through Schoharie, but as Tufts was wounded during the attack on the Middle Fort, one must, of course place doubt on the story. At any rate, Murphy, Tufts, Joseph Evans and Joachim Folluck, who were probably continual scouting companions, went over the hills of Summit. Murphy, by some mishap, became separated from the others. This is the incident in which he supposedly managed to shoot down several pursuing Indians, clubbing one with his rifle, taking his gun. He amazed the Indians by firing both barrels of his double rifle, and made them believe he could shoot all day. As Murphy stated to his children he used his double rifle only for garrison duty, as it was rather heavy. Therefore great doubt must be shed on the entire story.[178]

Murphy's first biographer mentioned another adventure involving Tufts. On this occasion as "...himself, Follock, Tufts and Evans were passing through the woods, they saw 10 or 12 Canadians marching towards them in Indian file, with what appeared to be muskets on their shoulders. The four secreted themselves, until the Canadians got between them, when what appeared to be guns, were mere clubs of black birch. They all arose simultaneously and presenting, ordered them to surrender. Being unarmed (except with hunting knives), they complied, and very demurely marched to the American Camp."[179]

At some point after the war, Tufts returned to New Hampshire, and settled in the Cheshire area as a farmer. In his pension deposition of 1818, Tufts claimed to be in good health, living with his wife Mary, with two children still at home—Abigail, age 15, and Caleb, age 13, all healthy but living in "reduced circumstances." The net worth of his possessions were assessed at only $24.50.[180]

Recorded in a descriptive list of men raised in Middlesex Co., Mass., agreeable to a resolve of Dec. 2, 1780, can be found the following about a Zachariah Tufts: age, 21 years, stature, 5ft. 9 in., complexion, light, eyes, blue, occupation, laborer (also given farmer), engaged for town of Woburn, engaged April 1, 1781, term, 3 years. While this is almost certainly the same Tufts, the age does not agree with his pension age, but it does indicate that he may have left the Schoharie region before the end of the war. See *Massachusetts Soldiers and Sailors of the Revolutionary War*, Boston, 107, vol. XVI, p.140.

Joseph Evans (1760 ? - 1832 ?)

By the time he was twenty and had joined the Albany County Militia in 1780, Joseph Evans probably had seen more action, hard campaign duty and adventure than most soldiers twice his age. Born around 1760, Evans claimed to have seen six years of service in the Continental line, having joined the American army in 1774. After forty-five years, his memory served him wrong, as he could not have joined the army until 1775, indicating five years of service. Nonetheless, Evans probably had to lie about his age when he enlisted as a private in Captain Joseph Crockett's Company of Colonel McClanahan's Regiment (7th Virginia).[181]

According to his pension deposition, Evans fought at the Battle of Bound Brook, New Jersey, on April 13, 1777, (Palm Sunday), where a detachment of troops under General Benjamin Lincoln was pushed back past the Raritan River by a much superior number of British troops. In the winter of 1777 at Morristown, Joseph was drafted into Morgan's regiment of picked riflemen. On June 22, 1777, Morgan pushed down the Raritan, routed a German picket guard, and hotly pursued the enemy to Piscataway in a spirited action while

General Wayne's regulars, who were supposed to support
Morgan, barely caught up to give much help. After this, Evans participated in the magnificent actions of Morgan's Riflemen at Freeman's Farm (September 19, 1777) and Bemis
Heights (October 7, 1777). Soon after, Morgan's men made
a forced march back to the main army under Washington
which left only about 175 of the 500 riflemen fit for duty due
to illness, casualties, attrition and for many, simply the lack
of shoes. Among those fit for duty was Evans, indicating that
he was one of the really tough ones, even though only about
17 years old. The riflemen fought under Lafayette in an action near the Delaware River on the New Jersey side where
the Marquis, "charmed" with the riflemen, marveled at their
endurance. Morgan's men also fought at Edge Hill (or
Whitemarsh), Pennsylvania on December 7, 1777, and
earned General Washington's personal thanks for their "gallant behavior."

Evans probably went into winter quarters at Radnor, near
Valley Forge, where the rifle corps was posted. Unlike other
regiments, the riflemen took no winter respite from military
duties, as they continued constantly patrolling, spying upon
the enemy in Philadelphia, and apprehending Loyalist
farmers bringing produce into the city. Evans was with Morgan as they pursued Clinton's redcoats across the Jerseys in
the spring of 1778, and perhaps fought in the skirmishes
around Monmouth. Soon after this, Captains Parr and Long
were detached to the Schoharie frontier; Evans was in
Long's company, as a sergeant. Here he states he took part
in all "expeditions against the Indians," indicating he participated in the forced march and sacking of the Loyalist-
Indian towns of Unadilla and Onoquaga, (October, 1778),
the Onondaga expedition (April, 1779), and the Sullivan-
Clinton expedition (June-October, 1779). As a member of
Long's company, perhaps he was present at the ambush of

Captain Charles Smith's Loyalists along Schoharie Creek (August, 1778).[182]

After his enlistment expired in late 1779 or early 1780, Joe (as he is referred by the informal spelling of his name in Sigsby's *Timothy Murphy*), returned to Schoharie and rejoined his wife, Maria Becker, whom he had married on March 3, 1779, when she was 16. In Schoharie, Evans seems to have operated mainly out of the Upper Fort as a ranger or scout. During the attack on the Middle Fort, on October 17, 1780, Evans, along with Peter Swart and William Zimmer, were detached by Captain Jacob Hager from the Upper Fort to scout out the situation at the Middle Fort and see if it had fallen. This was a dangerous assignment as a thousand of the enemy were busy burning and plundering the central part of the valley. They sighted the American flag and returned to report the joyous news that the fort was still holding out.[183] In 1781-1783, Joseph served in Colonel Peter Vrooman's 15th Regiment of Albany County, and for a time also served in Colonel Morris Graham's Regiment of New York State Levies.[184]

In the many tales concerning Tim Murphy, the names of his friends are often encountered. One doubtful story, which has come down in the Murphy family, has the redoubtable Tim captured by a party of Indians, and, soon after, escaping. This was in the area of Springfield near Otsego Lake. When Murphy failed to return to the fort, David Ellerson and Joe Evans volunteered to go in search of him. Luckily they found him, just before a party of seven Indians attacked. Two of the enemy fell in the first fire. Murphy killed another with a tomahawk. Ellerson brought down another and when Evans was rendered *hors de combat*, Murphy seized his rifle. The remaining three Indians realized there was little chance of recapturing their prisoners and quickly fled.[185]

Members of the recreated unit, Captain Jacob Hager's Company of the 15th Regiment of Albany County, fire a salute over the graves of Revolutionary veterans near the site of the upper Fort. Photo by Leslie La Crosse.

Evans is also said to have been a member of the scout which, during the Indian campaign of 1779, shot an Indian out of a canoe on the Chemung River. On another occasion, Murphy, Evans, Tufts and Folluck went out on a scout in the vicinity of Summit. This was the time Murphy was pursued by a party of Indians, killing several of them. By firing both shots from his double rifle and a third from the gun of an Indian he had just killed, he made the Indians believe he could continually shoot without ever reloading. These four rangers are also credited with capturing a party of 10 or 12 Canadians at some point during the war.[186] Such are many of the undocumented stories of these men, tales which became part of the folklore of the region.

After residing in the Schoharie region for several years following the war, Evans moved to the Tennessee frontier. In

1820, Evans applied for his pension in Claiborne County, Virginia, at the age of 61. His holdings were assessed at $195.00, which makes him one of the more well-to-do of the riflemen, at least in later life. He was a farmer, could not read or write, had a "sickly" wife, age 58, and two daughters still at home, ages 18 and 16, the latter also in poor health. In 1830, Evans was still alive and well in Illinois, but evidently died two years later, as records disclose the death of a Joseph Evans from Virginia who was buried in his family's plot. He died on September 4, 1832.*

There is no mention of service in the War of 1812, but Evans was young enough at the time and would have been required to serve in the militia. But regardless of when or where he died, Joe Evans must have been one remarkable, tough and capable frontiersman who, in every way, measured up to his older counterparts in the rifle corps.

David Ellerson (1749 - 1838)

When reciting the long roll call of the many great riflemen of Revolutionary War fame, two names always stand above the great majority: Tim Murphy and Dave Ellerson. Many stories and legends surround this pair. Though they never wore epaulets, it is their names that are most remembered above all the other soldiers and militiamen. We are indebted to Ellerson (also spelled Elerson, Ellison, Allison, etc.) for much of what we know about the riflemen, as he

---

* His gravesite can be found in Kirkland Cemetery, Borento, Bond County, Illinois, where it is marked by a government headstone. Evans evidently came to Illinois in 1818, and settled in Seminary Township, Fayette County. See *Soldiers of the American Revolution Buried in Illinois*, Springfield, 1975, p.71.

lived long enough to relate their adventures to Jeptha Simms, the great chronicler of the border wars.

Ellerson was a Scotsman, born en route to Virginia on October 14, 1749, and lived in Culpeper County.[187] He may have been something of a "long hunter," those men who were among the first whites to traverse the vast region west of the Alleghenies. We find him involved in the early Indian wars of western Virginia, including the Battle of Point Pleasant (in present-day West Virginia) during Lord Dunmore's War in 1774. During that bloody engagement with the Shawnees, Ellerson obtained a flanking position on the enemy. Although in great peril and shot through the left shoulder, one or two effective shots successfully persuaded the Indians to abandon their position.[188]

In 1775, the Culpeper Minutemen were instrumental in running Loyalist Governor Lord Dunmore out of Virginia. Ellerson was possibly one of them. He may also have served at the Battle of Great Bridge, Virginia, a significant victory for the riflemen. In the fall of 1776, he entered military service for three years, and was with Washington's troops when they crossed the Delaware and captured Trenton on December 26, and was at the victory at Princeton on January 3, 1777. In the following winter at Morristown, New Jersey, David became a member of Morgan's picked riflemen, serving in Captain Gabriel Long's company. He fought in many skirmishes throughout central New Jersey and was sent with Morgan's riflemen to the northern army and fought at Saratoga in September and October of 1777. One legend states that David with his inseparable companion and lifelong buddy, Tim Murphy, actually penetrated the British lines and captured an enemy officer and sentry.[189]

More than likely, Ellerson saw service at Whitemarsh (December 7, 1777), Valley Forge (1777-1778) and Barren Hill (May 20, 1778). After the Monmouth battle, Morgan and his "shirtmen" hung on the tails of the retreating British army, pursuing them toward Raritan Bay, where Ellerson, Murphy, William Leek, and John Wilbur were granted a request by Morgan to reconnoiter ahead. David actually penetrated to the beach as the enemy was embarking from Gravelly Point, effecting a landing on Staten Island. Near the Middletown shore he attempted to capture a coach. Ellerson, in effect, made it known to a nearby dragoon to either surrender himself or be gone. After finding the surf too strong to swim his horse out to his comrades, the dragoon returned and attempted to pull out his pistol, but Ellerson was faster and shot him out of his saddle. This was just the confrontation David hoped to avoid as it alerted the enemy fleet. A sentry, had, upon seeing Ellerson, panicked and dropped his musket into the water. David compelled the man to drive the carriage for him just as cannon fire began to tear up the beach around them. With his prisoner at the reins, Ellerson made his way back to the American army, riding in high style. Supposedly, this coach belonged to Sir Henry Clinton. Ellerson claimed he sold it for $178.00, which he sent to his ailing father in Virginia.[190]

Just after this incident, his company, along with Captain James Parr's company, was sent to the Schoharie Valley to protect the inhabitants of that beleaguered frontier. Some of Captain Long's Company were soon detached to intercept a party of Loyalists under Captain Charles Smith coming up Schoharie Creek. After capturing enemy runners carrying intelligence from Joseph Brant to Christopher Service of a party of Loyalists under Smith coming up the stream, Long deployed his men for an ambush. According to Ellerson's account recorded by Simms, Long was to be allowed to fire first at Smith, but in case he missed, it would then be David's chance. In the well researched novel, *The Riflemen*, by John Brick, Long and Ellerson placed bets on who would get the Loyalist leader—in the unlikely event that it is true, Ellerson lost as Long shot Smith through the head. A few more Tories may have been wounded while the rest were soon dispersed—the first offensive action against the enemy in this quarter of the frontier. Long sent Smith's scalp to General Stark in Albany. A detachment of riflemen had been sent to the home of Service to apprehend him, if possible. Ellerson stated he was on both of these scouts, though there is some question of which event occurred first and if David could have been on both. According to the generally accepted story, Service attempted to resist by swinging at Tim Murphy with an axe. Murphy avoided the blow and shot the Tory dead.[191]

Ellerson may have participated in the raid and sacking of Onoquaga and Unadilla in October, 1778, under Colonel William Butler of the 4th Pennsylvania and Major James Parr of the rifle corps. This campaign was waged under the most trying conditions, but was successful, as these places were important launching spots for Indian-Loyalist raids. In November, Butler's Rangers and Brant's Indians retaliated by attacking Fort Alden in the Cherry Valley, which they failed to take. The Schoharie troops got there in time only to bury those murdered in the massacre. Also, as a member of Long's Company, Ellerson likely took part in the raid and sacking of the Onondaga towns in April, 1779.

In June of 1779, the 4th Pennsylvania and the rifle corps were sent up the Mohawk River in bateaux, landing near Canajoharie, they rendezvoused with the troops under General Clinton preparing for the expedition to sack the Indian country of western New York. While a road was being built from there to Otsego Lake, a rifle officer, unnamed, sent his servant for the day, David Ellerson, to a deserted house to gather some greens. Ellerson said this was in June. The journals kept on the expedition concur with this and document it to be Sunday, June 27, probably starting about 11 a.m. At this house, David was discovered by nearly a dozen Iroquois warriors. He immediately seized his rifle, which he had left carelessly leaning against the building, when several tomahawks were hurled at him, one nearly severing a finger. He dropped his haversack of greens and fled, jumped over a fence and several deadfalls, plunging into the woods just as the Indians, fearing that he might escape, fired their muskets at him. However, their balls only rattled the timber around him. Driven away from the camp, he ran on and on, not knowing whither to go. After running for several hours, he thought he had eluded his pursuers and stopped to rest. Just then, an Indian appeared in front of him. Ellerson meant to shoot him just as a shot from behind entered his body just above the hip, giving him a bad flesh wound. He changed his direction and continued his flight.

He crossed a cool stream and scooped up some water in his hands and drank. He felt somewhat more invigorated, but proceeding a short distance further, he felt faint and threw himself behind a fallen tree just as the lead Indian appeared. Up to now Ellerson had refrained from firing, realizing that one shot was all that might have kept back the enemy. But now, sure of his fate, bleeding badly, and wounded in two places, he resolved not to die unavenged. Too weak to hold his rifle, he sat down, rested it upon his knees, fired, and killed the warrior. Barely completing the process to reload his piece, the other Indians soon appeared. Preparing to bring down another, he relented, as the Indians gathered around what had been their fallen leader and began to chant their death wail, thereby giving the bewildered rifleman another unexpected chance to escape. He slipped further into the forest, lost his trail in a winding stream and came upon a large hollow hemlock tree into which he crawled and fell asleep. After three nights and two days in his gloomy shelter without food or water or having his wounds dressed, he crept from his place of concealment, cold, stiff, and hungry. By the sun's rays he directed his course and came to a place near Cobleskill, also known as Brown's Mills, about 3 miles from his place of hiding and at least 25 miles from the place where he had been surprised. Captain Christian Brown, who knew the shirtman, treated him kindly and sent him to the Middle Fort some 10 miles on where he eventually recovered. Although this great race for life is less known than a number of others in frontier annals, among which is the September 1778, one by John Adam Helmer, who is credited with warning the inhabitants of German Flats, or John Colter's much celebrated run from the Blackfeet around 1809, it is, in some ways, even more spectacular. While the unhurt Helmer threw away his gun to escape and Colter only ran 6 miles before eluding his captors, Ellerson was not only wounded and retained his rifle (or so he told Simms), he even killed the leader of his pursuers before escaping. Other runs of riflemen include William Leek's run from a large party of Loyalists and Indians on August 9, 1780; Hoever's run the same day; and Tim Murphy's run from the horde of enemy rangers and Indians who attacked Boyd's scouting detachment near Conesus Lake on September 13, 1779. But none can compare to the one by Ellerson from Springfield to Cobleskill.[192]

In his pension deposition, Ellerson stated he was discharged in present Otsego County in the fall of 1779, his enlistment having expired. He remained in Schoharie and was joined by at least nine other riflemen who also returned. Six of them, including Ellerson, enlisted in Captain Bogart's company of Colonel Harper's regiment in the spring of 1780, serving until November 1st of that year,[193] where they operated as scouts or rangers.

Ellerson and Murphy were two of the greatest scouts of the northeast, having had numerous adventures. One legend has Ellerson, Murphy, and Joe Evans wiping out a band of 7 Indians. No doubt they had a multitude of hair-raising encounters never recorded.

During Sir John Johnson's campaign to raze the Schoharie Valley in the fall of 1780, Ellerson participated in the defense of the Middle Fort, garrisoned by some 204 Continentals and militia. There, a detachment consisting of Murphy, Ellerson, Leek, Hoever, Wilbur, Tufts, and Lloyd of the riflemen, along with several other local rangers and volunteers, encountered the 1,000 man force of Indians, Loyalists, British, and Hessians. A delaying action was attempted. So close and hot was the skirmish that several received bullet holes in their hunting frocks. Not until the fence they had taken cover behind was riddled with bullet holes, did the rangers retire, without any losses. One account states that one man, Samuel Reynolds, mounted the highest point in the fort and exposed his hind parts to the enemy. However, an enemy marksman, possibly on order from Johnson himself, took aim and shot him, tumbling him to the ground where he broke his neck and died. Ellerson had command of a small body of rangers that day and made a sortie in an effort to prevent the Indians from burning a nearby barn. After shooting both a Loyalist or a British officer as well as an Indian (whose body was found later where he had crawled off and died), David found himself alone and some distance from the fort. As he dashed across the clearing, a full 700 of the enemy were said to have blazed away at this lone figure, and they all missed! It was indeed a narrow escape, as several bullets passed through his hunting shirt. Perhaps it is noteworthy that if the story is true, Ellerson could hit his target with little difficulty, and several hundred of the foe could not.[194]

The commander of the fort, Major Melancthon Woolsey, evidently attempted to allow a flag of truce to enter the fort. Every time it approached, however, Murphy fired on it while, at nearly the same time, kept the major at bay (possibly with his double barreled rifle). Ellerson faithfully backed up his comrade's insubordination, for, as he would later explain to Simms, they both had extra prices on their scalps and suspected that Woolsey would surrender the fort. With a near mutiny on his hands, Woolsey allowed himself to be relieved of command, the charge of which fell to the spirited Colonel Peter Vrooman.[195] Quite possibly the preventive actions of Murphy, Ellerson, and several other riflemen, were responsible for saving the Middle Fort.

Ellerson was closely connected to the other riflemen and probably served with them when they enlisted in captain

Jacob Hager's company of the 15th Regiment of Albany County Militia. In May 1781, he enlisted in Captain Peter Van Rensselaer's company of Colonel Marinus Willett's regiment of New York levies, and was discharged on December 31, 1781.[196] His name is also found among the names of the militia of Ulster County.

At some point during his service in Schoharie, Ellerson made the acquaintance of Sara Beagraft, a widow with a young son. She was evidently from Lunenburg, Germany, and had come to America by way of Boston. She saw Ellerson's run to the Middle Fort in 1780, according to Simms. They were married on December 15, 1780. Sara died in 1830.[197] About 1785, he and his family moved to a spot near the Platten Kill, now in the town of Gilboa, settling on part of the 600-acre tract that he had been rewarded for his services in the war. The Ellerson house, a small frame dwelling, still stands. Behind it is an old tree, which was evidently used as a target. About 15 or 20 feet above the ground, in a scarred area, numbers of rifle balls have been found. The museum at the "Old Stone Fort," near Schoharie, has several relics which reputedly belonged to the famous ranger, including some shot pouches and a captured Hessian bayonet. Mr. Allen Burton, of Gallupville, has in his possession a rifle that allegedly belonged to Ellerson. It came down through his family and is believed to have been made by Jacob Palm. That the rifle was actually Ellerson's is supported by tax records for the years 1767 - 1777, and indicates it to be an extremely rare New York State rifle. Esopus was in Ulster County, not all that far from David's neighborhood. But whether it was the piece he carried throughout his many adventures and forays during the war is another question, though the rifle is of the early Revolutionary War period. In 1777, when Morgan's men were returning from Saratoga, a rifle demonstration was supposedly given. Ellerson's rifle was said to have been one of the finest in the regiment. He gave it to a man by the name of John Garsaway (later on duty in Schoharie), to take a shot, scoring a perfect hit at 100 yards and killing the sapling behind it. The owner of the tree was delighted and amazed at the skill of the riflemen.[198]

After the war, Ellerson followed the business of farming and no doubt supplemented his family's fare by hunting. On occasion, he rejoined his old comrades from the rifle corps for shooting matches, which his buddy, Tim Murphy, usually won. The Ellersons are said to have had 13 children. David and Sara were married for a half-century until her death in 1830. The old scout was interviewed by Josiah Priest and Jeptha Simms, and having lived to a ripe old age, as did most of the Schoharie riflemen, he received his pension (of which his ownings were assessed at $57.13). Upon his death in 1838, he was buried in the Flat Creek cemetery, where there is a monument to him.[199] There is also a plaque dedicated to him at the Old Stone Fort.

Said to have been tall, lean, and athletic, David had blue eyes. He finished his years bearing the scars of war.

Timothy Murphy, Legends vs. Facts (1751 - 1818)

Almost without doubt, of the ten riflemen who returned to the Schoharie region, Timothy Murphy is the most famous, and the most famous private soldier of the entire Revolution. With much justification he should rank right up there with other great American war heroes like Alvin York or Audie Murphy. Like the other riflemen, he fought throughout the entire war, no small feat in itself.

"Sure-shot Tim,"[200] as one contemporary officer actually referred to him, was present at some of the most important moments of the war and racked up a most spectacular war record. The siege of Boston, disaster at Long Island, crossing the Delaware with Washington, the surrender of Burgoyne, Valley Forge and the surrender of Cornwallis, are but a few.

Murphy was the subject of a great deal of myth-making during the 19th century. In the twentieth century he, like virtually all folk heroes, underwent a great deal of debunking by those who seem to get a sadistic pleasure out of toppling heroes off their pedestals. Riflemen, in general, have also undergone vicious belittling in recent times. Some historians have attempted to downplay the role of Murphy and the riflemen, even at battle sites such as Saratoga. This is perhaps as a reactionary viewpoint to the overly glorious viewpoint of the earlier authorities. But when the smoke clears and the swinging pendulum comes to rest at its proper perspective, the role of the riflemen will be seen for the impressive one it truly was. While some contemporaries may term them as "absolutely worthless;" as one historian told the author, it is the great number of early accounts, especially those of the enemy, that will more than acquit them. Painstaking research, presented here, will hopefully clarify the true worth of Murphy, the man.

No biography, in the strictest sense of the word, is presented here. Two books have already covered that. Most of the material on Murphy can be found in *Timothy Murphy, Hero of the Revolution,* by Sigsby, *The Frontiersmen of New York* and *Schoharie County and Border Wars,* by Simms, *History of Schoharie County,* by Roscoe, *History of Delaware County,* by Gould, and *What Manner of Men,* by Cook. There are also several novels which include Murphy. Except for O'Brien and Simms, most accounts accept all of the legends, many of which are questionable. Most of the Murphy stories can perhaps be put into three categories: those of a Paul Bunyan stature, which are humanly and physically impossible; those concerning individual exploits, often involving his double-barreled rifle, and are now impossible to decipher as fact or fiction; and those that are documented fact. With the facts presented, Murphy needs no polishing by myth-makers, for the truth by itself is even more fascinating.

LEGEND: Murphy killed a whole boatload of redcoats stuck on a shoal, during the siege of Boston in 1775.

FACT: Probably not. Murphy was present as one of Thompson's riflemen during the siege of Boston. This account of a rifleman calmly picking off a boatload of regulars safely outside of musket range was reported in a paper at the time. There were 1400 riflemen encamped at Cambridge at the time. One of the reasons actually giving Murphy the credit for the deed is nonsense; only a double-barreled rifle with a conical bullet could have reached that far (nearly a half mile). Such a piece has no more range than a single barreled rifle. Conical shaped bullets were not in use at the time. That the entire boatload of redcoats were all shot by a single rifleman is quite possibly true, but the distance was probably exaggerated by the time the papers got hold of the story. The odds are 1400 to 1 it was Tim.

LEGEND: Murphy shot General Simon Fraser at Saratoga, from a distance of 300 yards.

FACT: Quite possibly. Many historians have argued this question for some time, and those at Saratoga battlefield have a tendency to discredit the legend as a 19th-century myth, claiming it might have been a man, who, when quite elderly, stated he shot Fraser with his fowler. But it is a weak story at best and full of holes. Three accounts, two contemporary and one second hand, written by the three most likely to know, are among the only descriptions to agree in the details. These are a British soldier's account of Fraser's death, Colonel Daniel Morgan's relating of the event to both a British officer a few years later and during an address to Congress in the late 1790's, and Murphy's own account to his children.[201] All three agree that it was a man by himself who did it, that he was a rifleman, and that he was posted in a tree. The Morgan and Murphy accounts both agree that only one individual was selected for the rather nasty job, and that after climbing a tree, quickly accomplished it with the first shot. (Legends have Murphy finally killing Fraser on his third attempt). Murphy was said to take offense when anyone asked how many shots it took, as if his marksmanship was being questioned. Morgan said he ordered one of his best shots to do it, and evidence abounds that Murphy, who two years later was stated as being well known to the officers of the army, was well known for his marksmanship during the war.

Also, General Edward Hand, who, it would seem, knew Murphy personally, introduced him to General Washington on his upstate tour in 1783. Why would a private, illiterate rifleman and scout be presented to the commander-in-chief unless he had accomplished a great deed? Murphy was certainly not the only adventure-seeking rifleman of the war. A more important reason must be sought. And Murphy's mutiny at the Middle Fort in 1780 would hardly qualify him as the sort of soldier to introduce to Washington.

Some have even stated that Murphy was not even present at the battles of Saratoga. Indeed, a number of the riflemen were sick, leaving Morgan with about 350 men. Muster rolls were not always accurate. Murphy had been drafted into Morgan's regiment a short time before the northern campaign. A payroll has been found for Morgan's riflemen present on the field at the time and Murphy's name was one of them. Others have stated that Murphy's regiment at the time (the 3rd Pennsylvania) was elsewhere and that he must have been with it. This is based on ignorance of the rifle corps however, as the men were picked from various regiments to be on detached duty, although still officially a part of their original unit. Morgan himself was considered a member of the 11th Virginia, also not present at Saratoga.

This author believes, with all excuses aside, that the evidence points to Murphy as the slayer of General Fraser.

LEGEND: Murphy had a double-barreled rifle.

FACT: Apparently True! Although long-questioned by many if such a rifle was used at all by Murphy, the proof has evidently been found. Many have questioned if such rifles were in use at the time, but the evidence is so strong as to nail it down almost without doubt. Double-barreled rifles date back to the 17th century in Europe, and did exist at the time of the American Revolution. Although uncommon at the time, they were not necessarily unusual. In Simms' *Frontiersmen of New York*, he noted that a son of Murphy's informed him that he had often heard his father say more was said about his double-barreled rifle than it merited. This would seem a truthful statement, because if Murphy were given to boasting or lying, it is unlikely he ever would have underestimated his rifle. His son informed Simms he did have such a gun, but it was so heavy he seldom used it except on garrison duty. This would indicate that on scout, Tim probably used a single-barreled rifle like the others.

But there is more evidence. Mr. Allen Burton, a collector of Revolutionary War rifles and accouterments, has a page taken from the account book of Isaac Worly, a riflesmith at Easton, Pennsylvania. In it, along with a list of other rifles made, is the following transaction for his business of 1776:

"Feby – 19th a Rifle Made for Timothy Murphy a Two barrel rifle – both barrels Rifled only one made"

His rifle was not made by John Golcher, as has been often stated. In February 1776, Murphy's regiment (Colonel Hand's riflemen) was still stationed at Cambridge, Massachusetts. The order may have been placed when his company passed through Easton in June 1775, on their way to Boston. Worly had a great number of orders then, probably due to the war. So, it would seem, except on the chance of the document being an amazingly good fake, that Murphy did indeed possess a "Two barrel Rifle."

The museum at the Old Stone Fort owns a photograph, taken in the 1930's, of a man holding a rifle, supposedly Murphy's. It is an early looking style without a patchbox, and appears devoid of most decoration; in short, a down to earth, no nonsense, single-barreled rifle. If it truly is Murphy's, then in some ways it is even more valuable than his double-barreled piece, for it could be the one he carried on his many campaigns and forays against the enemy. Unfortunately, its whereabouts are unknown today, though it is believed to possibly be in Florida.[202]

So it would seem that although Tim probably did not use an "over and under" rifle to kill Fraser at Saratoga, he evidently did have one and perhaps used it to great advantage during the attack on the Middle Fort on October 17, 1780. The stories persisting he used the double barreled gun on his various forays and scouts against the Indians probably arose from people seeing or hearing about his double rifle who assumed he used it all the time.

LEGEND: Murphy saved the Middle Fort by firing on the enemy flag party and actually threatened to shoot his commander if he allowed the party to enter.

FACT: True. Murphy and Ellerson both had extra prices on their scalps at the time and well knew their fate if ever taken alive, according to Ellerson's explanation to Simms. Both resolved to kill Major Melancthon Woolsey sooner than let the fort fall. Both Angelica Vroman and Ellerson told Simms the story and the pension depositions of Nicholas Rightor, Enos Howard, and probably others mention the incident. Colonel John Butler noted in his journal of that day that the garrison fired repeatedly on his flag party.

More pension accounts are bound to be found describing this incident. That is one of the great advantages to them as they can be used to counteract and verify each other.

LEGEND: Murphy was the only survivor of the Groveland massacre in 1779.

FACT: False, but only 7 or 9 did manage to break out or flee and Murphy was one of these. Probably he was a flanker and escaped at the opening fire, but Simms believed he might have been one of the three to break through at the last moment.

On September 13, 1779, Lt. Thomas Boyd, of Simpson's company, with 26 men (two had returned as runners), stumbled into several hundred of Butler's Rangers and Iroquois Indians under Butler and Brant. Fourteen were killed on the spot, three were captured (Boyd, Parker, and Hanyery, an Oneida chief, who was quickly killed) and two couriers had been previously dispatched to General Sullivan. Evidently, Murphy was pursued by the Indians, who failed to overtake him before he reached the main army. A couple of journals mention this escape, which could well have been his most hair-breadth getaway.

LEGEND: Murphy killed over 40 of the enemy and scalped many of them.

FACT: Apparently true. A journal for September 13, 1779, said that after Murphy made it to the American camp in his escape from the ambuscade near Genesee, he had killed his "third and thirtieth" enemy. It also stated he was well-known to the officers. Murphy could easily have increased his score to 40 or more by 1783, during the years he was best remembered for his exploits. It is well-known that Murphy, like many other riflemen, often scalped his fallen foe. Of the 10 riflemen known to have returned to Schoharie, only 1 was killed and 2 wounded, but it would be interesting to know how many of the enemy were killed by them in return. Undoubtedly it was quite high, all the more amazing when we consider the fact that the Loyalists and Indians killed many more of the militia, in general, than vice-versa. No wonder these riflemen were welcomed back with open arms by the settlers in Schoharie!

Chronology Of Events In Tim Murphy's Life:

born 1751, near Minisink, N.J.

1759–family moves near Sunbury, Pa.

1773–axeman for surveying party; apprenticed to Van Campen family at about this time.

June, 1775–with his brother John and William Leek, enlists in Capt. Lowdon's Co., Thompson's Rifle Batt.

June–July–march to Boston.

Sept.–credited with killing boatload of enemy at a range of near half of mile.*

August, 1776–skirmishing on Long Is.

August 27–Battle of Long Island.

Fall–retreat across New Jersey.

Dec. 26–Battle of Trenton, N.J.

Jan. 2, 1777–delaying action to Trenton.

Jan. 3–Battle of Princeton, N.J.

Winter–Morristown encampment.

July 1777–drafted into Morgan's Rifle Corps (Parr's Co.) Skirmishing in New Jersey.

September–skirmishing near Saratoga, N.Y.

September 19–Battle of Freeman's Farm.

Oct. 7–Battle of Bemis Heights–is credited with killing both Fraser and Sir Francis Clerke.* Murphy and Ellerson credited with capture of officer and sentry.*

Dec. 7–Edge Hill (Whitemarsh), Pa.

July 31–first detachment reaches Middle Fort (via Albany). August–destruction of Capt. Smith's Loyalist, kills Christopher Service.*

Sept.–scout near present-day Arkville. Parents killed by Tories and Indians in Pennsylvania.

Oct.–sacking of Unadilla and Oquaga.

Nov.–leads scout along Mohawk River between Utica and Schenectady–they kill 3 Indians, then split up and flee.*

Spring, 1779–rescues girl and kills 4 Indians.*

Spring–numerous scouts.

June 27–Ellerson's run from the Indians.

June–scouts around Otsego Lake.

August 29–Battle of Newtown, rifle corps detects ambuscade.

August–September–over 40 Indian towns destroyed.

August–rifle stolen by Tory boy recovered.*

Sept. 13–reconnoiters Gaghsuquilahery, scalps Indian (33rd enemy); survives Genesee ambush; kills Indian using hat trick*; Boyd and Parker tortured.

Sept.–Rifle Corps among troops detached to destroy Indian towns east of Cayuga Lake.

November–Rifle Corps disbanded near West Point.

Late 1779-1780–returns to Schoharie.
  –rescues 2 men and his party kills 6 Indians.*
Oct.–marries Margaret Feeck against her father's (probably
   justified) wishes; wedding reception interrupted by
   scout reporting Indians; party resumed in fort.
Oct. 3-16–scout of rangers captures one Tory and returns to
   Middle Fort night before attack.
Oct. 17–attack on Middle Fort; Tim leads sorties, fires on
   flag party, refuses to let commandant surrender
   fort.–nearly all houses and barns burned
   –rebels sally out and burn Tory homes.
April, 1781–reenlists in army (3rd Pa.), evidently as a rifleman.
Summer–skirmishing with Tarleton in Va.; July–Battle of
   Green Springs.
October–present at seige of Yorktown.
Nov.–rejoins militia as ranger; at skirmishes at Bouck's Island and Lake Utsayantha under Capt. Hager. At latter again threatens to kill an officer for cowardice
   (for leaving Hager's rangers to do the fighting.)
Winter 1781-1782–spends time hunting in mountains
   around Schoharie tanning hides.
1782–numerous scouting.
1782 or 1783–possibly tracks down and kills Seth's Henry,
   who, according to Simms, may have killed more settlers than any other Indian on the frontier.*
1784–saves neighbor from drowning.
1780's–becomes mill owner; credited with killing revenge-
   seeking Indian with his own gun.
Early 1800's–stumps for William Bouck, famous politician.
1807–marries 27-year-old Mary Robertson, who is pregnant.
   –moves to Otsego County.
1818–dies of cancer of the throat.

*not documented; not all Murphy stories are included.

John Wilbur

It is unfortunate that we do not know more about John Wilbur (Williber). This account is based mainly on Simms' history, a few muster rolls, and references to the histories of his particular units. His birthplace is unknown, but he was from Reddington, Pennsylvania, and was a carpenter by trade.[203]

Wilbur was a member of Captain James Parr's Company, of the rifle regiment, and probably saw service in the many skirmishes and scouting parties in New Jersey; he was also at Saratoga and Valley Forge in 1777 and 1778. He was with the rifle corps when Morgan pursued the British in their retreat across the Jerseys in June and July 1778. It was at this time that Murphy, Ellerson, Tufts and Wilbur, four of the elite corps' aces, asked and obtained permission to pursue the enemy on their own hook to Raritan Bay. Morgan let them go with a warning of caution and to observe extreme vigilance. This illustrates how adventurous and danger-seeking these four were. This was the incident in which Ellerson allegedly captured the enemy coach right from under the enemy's nose!

After this, the companies of Captains James Parr and Gabriel Long, under Major Thomas Posey, along with Colonel William Butler's 4th Pennsylvania, were sent by Washington to support the Schoharie frontier against increasing Loyalist and Indian attacks. As one of the riflemen, it is probable Wilbur was active on the Unadilla-Onoquaga campaign against the Onondagas. His name is found among those on the Sullivan-Clinton campaign in the following year. Wilbur was back in Schoharie by May 1780, for on the first of that month we find him enlisted as a private in Captain Bogart's Company, Colonel Harper's Regiment, and here, with several of his comrades from the rifle corps, was listed as a rifleman and probably served in the capacity of a scout or ranger. In September 1780, most of Bogart's company was stationed at Fort Schuyler (Stanwix), to reinforce the 1st New York Regiment, plagued by desertions; however, six men listed as "Bogart Rifleman" were to remain at the Middle Fort.[204] Why this came about is unknown, perhaps the scouting abilities of the men were thought to be to better advantage if they stayed in the region, but regardless, as events would turn out, it was certainly to Schoharie's advantage they remained.

In October 1780, Sir John Johnson and Joseph Brant led about 1,000 British, Loyalists, Indians and Germans on a mission of destruction through the valley. Wilbur was one of the party under Major Eckerson of the militia, which, with 12 or 14 riflemen and Rangers, attempted to delay the enemy force from behind a board fence. Only after the fence was pierced with a great number of bullet holes, did the Americans retire to the fort. Wilbur was active in firing on the enemy through the stockade's loopholes and made several sorties. Simms has left us with an interesting anecdote of one such sortie. Ellerson had command of a small body of rangers, of which Wilbur was a member. As he fell in with a man in Indian garb catching a horse, Wilbur "...asked him to what party he belonged? He replied, 'the Indian party' and instantly received a bullet from Wilbur's rifle. He took off his scalp and as he entered the fort with it in his hand, Major Woolsey told him he ought to have his scalp taken off."[205] This man and another shot during the day were thought to be Indians but proved to be "blue-eyed Indians" (Loyalists), from the Albany area. When Murphy threatened to kill Woolsey if he attempted to discuss surrender terms with the enemy, the other riflemen, 6 or 7 strong (not counting the local rangers), almost certainly including Wilbur, rallied to his side, thus helping to save the Middle Fort. Shortly, Woolsey was relieved of command, so if Wilbur was afraid of being further chastised for the scalp, he no longer needed to worry.[206]

Along with several of the other riflemen, Wilbur is recorded to have signed up with Captain Jacob Hager's Company, 15th Regiment of Albany County Militia. As he seems to have served as a ranger, he must have had many untold adventures, now lost forever. In 1781, he entered Captain Benjamin Dubois' Company as a sergeant, and in 1782 we find him enrolled in Captain Joseph Harrison's Company of Colonel Willett's Regiment, again as a sergeant.[207] At some point during the war Wilbur married "a Miss Mattice."[208] Women seem to have been the principle reason these riflemen returned to Schoharie, although the breakup of the rifle corps in November 1779, and the expiration of their enlistments, must be considered as possible reasons also.

After the war, date unknown, Wilbur and his wife moved further west and settled on the Charlotte River, perhaps in the vicinity of the ill-fated Loyalist, Christopher Service. In a rifle match held in 1799 (see William Leek's biography), there was a fourth contestant not identified, who might well have been Wilbur.

Unfortunately, Wilbur left no pension account, probably dying before he could have applied (circa 1820). I have not found where he was born, his age, or when he died. He briefly emerges from the depths of history, tantalizing us with a few recorded facts, and then disappears.

William Lloyd

William Lloyd, a Virginian, led what must have been a dangerous, action-filled life. He undoubtedly participated in many a battle and skirmish as a member of the rifle corps, and evidently conducted scouts. Simms mentioned his rank as a sergeant, although muster rolls indicate him to have been a private. It is quite possible he rose to the rank of sergeant, perhaps in the Continental army, and that it was respected, off the record, by his comrades. As of now, it must be regarded as one of the minor details of Simms' histories, that remains questionable.

Unfortunately, little is known of him except passing references by Simms and the appearance of his name on muster rolls. However, just being a member of Morgan's partisans assures us of his abilities, as they were all picked riflemen, considered experts. As a Virginian, it is likely he enlisted in the 11th Virginia in the fall of 1776 or the winter of 1777, when Morgan brought them to Morristown, New Jersey. Here he served with David Ellerson, Joseph Evans, Lt. Elijah Evans, as well as other noteworthy Virginians who have come to our attention.

In all probability, ruling out the possibilities of detached duty, illness, furloughs, etc., Lloyd must have seen service in the constant skirmishing in New Jersey in the spring and summer of 1777, the Saratoga campaign in the fall, and perhaps the actions around Philadelphia in December. However, in these latter actions a great number of the riflemen were not involved, because of fatigue, casualties, general attrition, and most simply, having no shoes to continue.

The rifle corps, temporarily under Major Thomas Posey, was stationed at Radnor, near Valley Forge, in the winter of 1777-1778, and the men were often sent out to scout, spy, and harass the enemy, notably the German Jaegers (riflemen), detached by the enemy for the same purposes. As the rifle corps was a special regiment and not supported by any state, Washington made sure they were among the first troops to receive what scanty allowance of clothing there was. The corps fought commendably at Barren Hill, Pennsylvania in the spring. As the British abandoned Philadelphia and retreated towards New York, the riflemen kept on their rear, cutting up patrols, taking prisoners, and attempting to prevent enemy foraging parties from ravaging the countryside.

Lloyd was a member of Captain Gabriel Long's company, which was sent to Schoharie, along with Captain Parr's company, under Captain Commandant Thomas Posey, and Lt. Col. William Butler's 4th Pennsylvania, the first detachment arriving on July 31, 1778. Soon after their arrival in Schoharie, Butler sent out two parties: one party to apprehend Christopher Service (evidently including Tim Murphy, David Ellerson, and Zachariah Tufts); and another which spied upon the enemy at Unadilla. Lloyd may have been in the ambush of the detachment of Loyalists under Captain Charles Smith on the Schoharie River in early August 1778, and was likely with the rifle corps when they captured the double agent, Dumon, in September. He was perhaps among the 56 riflemen who were a part of the force that successfully wiped out the Tory-Indian rendezvous point at Unadilla. As Lloyd was in the company of Lt. Elijah Evans, he probably participated in the expedition against the sacking of Onondaga in April 1779.

After the Sullivan-Clinton expedition in 1779, and the expiration of his three-year enlistment (late 1779 or early 1780), Lloyd returned to Schoharie and enlisted as a private in Captain Bogart's Company of Colonel Harper's Regiment, on May 1, 1780. A number of his comrades also enlisted on that date. Kept separated, they were referred to as Bogart's riflemen. In September, this company was sent to Fort Schuyler (Stanwix) to reinforce the garrison, beset by dissatisfaction and desertion. However, six "Bogart Riflemen," including Lloyd, Murphy, Ellerson, Wilbur, Leek and Tufts, remained at the Middle Fort. One of these was a sergeant, possibly Lloyd, but it is not specified. [209]

A conch shell, used to assemble the rangers when they became separated in the woods, might have been carried by

Lloyd as Ellerson told Simms it was the leader who brought it on scout.

When, on October 1, 1780, Tim Murphy eloped with Peggy Feeck, he was accompanied by three of his friends, including Lloyd, who, on horseback helped to find the chilled Peggy after she waded the Schoharie, according to Simms. Soon after, the wedding party rode a wagon to Schenectady where the wedding ceremony was performed.

Shortly after their return, a scout was sent out consisting of Murphy, Bartholomew C. Vrooman (a local ranger), William Leek and Robert Hutt under (according to Simms) Sergeant Lloyd. This 13-day scout visited Punchkill, Sharon, Cherry Valley, Unadilla, Delhi, Minisink and Cairo. In short, it was a complete blanket around the west and south of the valley. It is incredible that such an area was covered in less than a fortnight. Reports had been coming in and it was believed something big was afoot. They saw the tracks of Indians, "sign" as it was called, though no Indians were seen. A Loyalist was captured near present-day Prattsville. As they were expected to be gone only eight or nine days, they were welcomed back with relief at the fort.[210]

The scout returned only the evening ahead of the great invasion of Johnson and Brant.

About daylight of October 17, 1780, the garrison of Continentals and militia heard three shots from the alarm gun from the Upper Fort and soon saw in the distance the light of burning buildings. A scouting party was ordered out to investigate the cause of the fires. Among these men were Lloyd, Murphy, Ellerson, Philip Hoever, Richard Hanson, Wilbur, Tufts, Leek, Adam Shell, Bartholomew C. Vrooman, Joachim Van Valkenburg, under Lt. Martinus Zeilie and Major Thomas Eckerson. These men, advancing toward the Upper Fort with caution, soon fell in with an advance party of Indians and commenced firing. After several minutes it became apparent that more Indians were attempting to outflank them. Eckerson wisely ordered a retreat as the enemy's entire force pursued the rangers. Outnumbered some 100 to 1, the scouts were the subject of a great deal of firing. Although bullets whistled through some of their hunting shirts, no one was hit. The commander, Major Melancthon Woolsey, attempted to parley with the enemy, but was prevented from doing so by Murphy who three times fired on the enemy flag party. When Woolsey ordered his arrest, he was prevented by the other riflemen, probably including Lloyd. Lloyd probably participated in the several sorties that day, in which Tufts was wounded in the shoulder and Ellerson barely escaped death as he made a dash for the sally port. The attack was lifted around 4 p.m., as Johnson advanced on the Lower Fort. At the latter, marksmen, perhaps riflemen, were posted in the tower of the stone church which still stands today, and wreaked havoc among the attackers.

Undoubtedly, Lloyd went out on many scouts, always in danger, probably having many untold adventures. It is still unknown how old he was, whom he married, where he lived, or when he died, but he is believed to have been closely connected with the Ellerson family near Gilboa, members of his family intermarrying with those of the latter. As no record was found of a marriage, Lloyd might well have taken a common-law wife, a not unusual arrangement at the time.

That William Lloyd could lead various scouts safely through the wilderness and have men like Murphy, Ellerson, and Leek follow him indicates the extremely high caliber of the man.

Note: We know relatively little about the following two men. However, as they are mentioned by Simms, it tells us they were remembered by some of the inhabitants as late as the 1830's and 1840's. They are listed on various muster rolls, but as they did not leave pension depositions, it may be thought that barring the slight possibility they felt they did not need them, they both died before 1817. We do not know when either was born, how long they lived, what they might have done before the war, and in the case of one, whom he might have married.

Felix Hoever

We do know Felix Hoever served in Captain Gabriel Long's company of Morgan's Rifle Corps, indicating he probably was a Virginian, as Long's company was nearly entirely composed of men from that state. He probably enlisted in late 1776 or early 1777, and was brought up to Morristown, New Jersey, in 1777. Undoubtedly, he saw action in skirmishes and battles there and likely at Saratoga. He was probably at Valley Forge and saw more fighting in Pennsylvania and later again in New Jersey. Along with the rifle corps, Hoever arrived in Schoharie in the summer of 1778. He probably went out on scouts and was perhaps in the Unadilla campaign of October 1778, and as one of Lt. Elijah Evans' men he was probably present on the Van Schaik expedition against the Onondagas in April 1779. He is listed in Captain Parr's company on a payroll for June 1779. Likewise, he would have been with the rifle corps at the Battle of Newtown, August 29, 1779, and again when they, along with several other regiments totaling 600 men, destroyed and burned the Cayuga villages on the eastern shore of the lake named for that nation.

In 1780, Felix was back in Schoharie and served in Captain Jeremiah C. Muller's company in Colonel Morris Graham's regiment of New York State Levies. In Schoharie, his name appears a few times in remembrances of the settlers.

Simms says Hoever, along with Conradt Winnie and William Leek, was dispatched by Captain Jacob Hager on August 9, 1780, on a scout, but does not tell us which Hoever. It may have been Philip, since his girlfriend was captured that day—more about that in the next biography. Felix was stationed at the Middle Fort when it was attacked on October 17, 1780. His role is unclear, but he may have been among the rangers who encountered the 1,000-man enemy force and fought a delaying action. Though heavily fired on, nobody was hit, and they made a successful withdrawal to the fort. He may have participated in one or more of the several sorties that day and likely was one of the riflemen who came to Murphy's and Ellerson's aid when they decided they would rather shoot their commander than be taken by the enemy.

He remained at Schoharie, but his service after November, 1780, when Graham's regiment was disbanded, is unknown.

Philip Hoever

Also a member of Captain Gabriel Long's company, and probably a Virginian, Philip Hoever's career is similar to that of Felix's, and as was common in those days, they may have enlisted together as brothers. This is especially probable as they both returned and enlisted in the local militia in Schoharie in 1780.

Philip was probably at Morristown in 1777, saw action in New Jersey, at Saratoga, in Pennsylvania, during the Monmouth campaign, and was among the troops stationed at Schoharie. His history is, no doubt, the history of the rifle corps. He may have been present during Captain Long's ambush of Loyalists in August 1778, Unadilla-Onoquaga in October 1778, Onondaga in April 1779, as well as numerous scouts. However, as his name does not appear on a muster roll for June 1779, he may not have been on Sullivan's Indian expedition, and may have been among a detachment of 15 riflemen ordered to remain at the Middle Fort.

He remained in Schoharie, probably because of the same reasons several of his comrades stayed—the lure of pretty Dutch and German girls. He enlisted as a private in Captain George Rightmyer's Company of Colonel Peter Vroman's 15th Regiment of Albany County. During his stay in Schoharie he made the acquaintance of Susannah Vroman (Vrooman), one member of that large group who inhabited the part of the valley appropriately known as "Vroomansland."[211]

On August 9, 1780, Captain Jacob Hager dispatched William Leek, Conradt Winnie and one of the Hoevers (Philip?) on a scout, the scout where Leek shot the Tory at what became known as "Dead Man's Creek." The location is near the western part of the present town of Fulton, later called Byrnville, or Sap Bush Hollow, about five or six miles from the Upper Fort. Immediately after the shooting, a large party of Indians, including Joseph Brant himself, and Seth's Henry, gave chase and very hotly pursued them. Hoever had to drop his knapsack containing valuable articles to outrun the Indians, while the latter, so intent to capture the rangers, did not even stop to loot it. (Hoever later recovered it intact). They were so closely followed that they separated, either by accident or design (a commonly resorted to tactic); Leek flying for his life towards the fort, while Hoever and Winnie were driven into the woods in an opposite direction. Hoever and Winnie somehow shook off pursuit and from a place of concealment near the Schoharie (at the present town of Blenheim), witnessed burnings and the prisoners and plunder being taken by the enemy. Among the Indians were a few white renegades who allegedly outdid the Indians in committing atrocities. If this Hoever was Philip, he must have been especially exasperated as one of the prisoners was Susannah Vroman. Five civilians were killed, 30 taken prisoner and nine dwellings and barns burned, including Colonel Vroman's. The dead were buried on Johannes Feeck's farm where their headstones can be found today. One can only imagine how perturbed Hoever might have been with Leek for firing, not to mention how Vroman felt with his home destroyed and his relatives carried off, or Hager whose explicit orders not to fire were disobeyed.[212]

Soon after this raid, Brant released most of the women and children captives who were returned to Schoharie on horseback, escorted by some Americans. Susannah was among this number. She was married to Philip the following winter, according to church records. Hoever was stationed at the Middle Fort when it was attacked. Perhaps he was in the sorties or rallied to Murphy's side when the latter threatened to kill Major Woolsey.

What Hoever may have done after this, or where he lived after the war, is at present unknown.

Summary

What more can be said about such a body of men? Man for man, there may be no comparable unit in American military history, and perhaps in the world! They were all above-average shots, as they were picked by Morgan's officers for their marksmanship from a number of regiments, and most fought throughout the entire war (something few soldiers could claim), which is more than adequate proof of their toughness and ability and luck to survive under unbelievable conditions. Many of these ten men were present at Valley Forge, both Morristown encampments and many of the most important campaigns of the war, surviving not only battles, but starvation and disease. At times, much of the army was nearly naked, so much so that some could not even leave their shelters. In fact, in December 1777, just before Valley Forge, most of Morgan's men were without shoes. The situation was the same as reported by Colonel William Butler when the rifle corps arrived in Schoharie in the summer of 1778. In those earlier days very little is known of their individual exploits, but simply the sheer numbers of events and places where they served assure us that they had scores of stories to tell. But it was from 1778 to 1782, when they served in upstate New York, that they really "banged" their way into history and folklore with Tim Murphy leading the way. It is often impossible to decipher fact from fancy and undoubtedly some of the wild stories told of Murphy and his companions are great exaggerations. However, they simply cannot be dismissed as some debunkers prefer, as there is invariably some truth beneath it all for the stories to have been told in the first place. In fact, some legends have been proven true. For example, we are now quite sure Murphy had a double-barreled rifle and the evidence is growing that it really was he who shot General Fraser at Saratoga.

These biographies have dealt with the facts and only brushed upon the legends. However, William L. Stone, in his *Life of Brant*, said of these hardy men that they were still fondly remembered by Schoharie's inhabitants for their many deeds of daring and heroism at the time of his writing in the 1830's. Schoharie's settlers, established and hard-working Dutch and German farmers, were often at a loss as how to deal with the enemy rangers and fierce Iroquois warriors. They were soon impressed with these riflemen, who boldly sallied forth into the dark and forbidding forest and fought the enemy in his own fashion, more often than not beating him at his own game, doing it just as ruthlessly. Occasionally, they were unsuccessful, such as the failure of the scout to report the presence of the enemy in time as on August 9, 1780, and instead fired on an enemy, or when Murphy himself led the rangers into an ambush at Bouck's Island in November 1781. The defeat at Lake Utsayantha was attributed more to the cowardice of the militia, and not to Captain Hager's men, who preformed admirably.

There are those who consider these men uneducated backwoods "bumpkins." Indeed, perhaps as many as two-thirds could be considered "illiterate," yet they were as educated to their lifestyle as any Ph.D. is to his today—and they knew how to stay alive. These expert woodsmen could read the woods as well as a scholar can read his books. They possessed practical knowledge, whether it was hunting, farming, building an adequate shelter, tracking and scouting, fighting or running away, as dictated by survival. They knew how to handle the rifle and were among the best marksmen in the world.

It is amazing these men survived the war as well as they did. Not counting the battles, campaigns, and winter encampments, take a quick look at their brushes with death.

When Murphy and 25 others were ambushed by 400 or more Loyalists and Indians, he still managed to break away and outstrip his pursuers. Or when Leek shot the Loyalist near Dead Man's Creek and outran the enemy, about 75 strong, for 9 or 10 miles right to the gates of the Upper Fort. Or the time when Ellerson made a mad dash to the Middle Fort and survived a blast of at least 700 muskets. The occasion when these men sallied from the Middle Fort, and firing from behind a board fence (riddled with bullet holes), were briefly outnumbered perhaps some 100 to 1, made it back through a hail of fire, some of which pierced the men's frocks and even hit a powder horn strap with yet not a ranger hit. Or when the Rangers were ambushed by Chrysler near Bouck's Island and only one man was hit at such close range. On at least five occasions these men outran the fleet-footed Indians (Murphy at least once, but likely on other occasions as well: Leek once, Hoever once, and Ellerson at least twice). These events were ones these men should not, by all rights, have survived.

Added up, these ten men had about 65 or 70 years of war-time experience between them. This is without counting the possible post-war Indian fighting of at least one, Joseph Evans, who by law would have been required to serve in the militia during the War of 1812, in either Tennessee or Illinois.

The damage these men wreaked upon the enemy may at first seem incredible. Once again ignoring the legends, let's take a look. Murphy was said to have killed over 40 of the enemy. A journal kept in 1779 mentioned his thirty-third victim, *before* the period of his greatest fame. Add to this the possible kills by Ellerson (who only briefly touched upon his most incredible adventures to two chroniclers), and there is a minimum of four more, though the real number must be considerably higher. It was remembered that Leek killed one, but quite possibly more fell to his sharpshooting,

Wilbur killed and scalped a "blue-eye Indian" near the walls of the Middle Fort, and a story claims Tufts may have shot Service, the Loyalist, at the same time Murphy did. Folktales frequently mention Tufts, Evans, and the "half blood," Folluck, crediting them with inflicting other losses on the enemy. Except for Murphy, individual exploits prior to the rifle corps' arrival in Schoharie, are largely unrecorded, yet each one was a veteran of most of the war's important engagements and campaigns in those three years. Consider that at the battle at Freeman's Farm in 1777, Morgan's 350 riflemen and Dearborn's 200 light infantry are credited with inflicting half or more of the 600 casualties suffered by the British and Germans. (If most of our men were present and were doing an average job, it would indicate another 5 to 10 casualties). Later, at Bemis Heights, the rifle corps again went to work and cut the enemy to pieces, killing a disproportionate number of officers. Plus, add in all the battles and skirmishes in which we can only speculate, and the final number must be tremendous. A possible breakdown of the losses inflicted and a conservative estimate might look something like this:

Murphy	40 plus
Ellerson	4 plus
Leek	1 plus
Wilbur	1 plus
Tufts	1 plus
	47 plus total
	3 plus prisoners
total	50 plus killed, wounded and captured.

The three prisoners is an extremely low estimate—the *Clinton Papers, Writings of Washington,* journals, and again, the multitude of legends, indicate many more taken, but the contemporary accounts are invariably silent on who those low ranking individuals were. Of the kills, at least six may have been of some importance: Murphy is credited with picking off both General Simon Fraser and Sir Francis Clerk at Saratoga (Fraser was second in command to Burgoyne. In fact, it was only through the greatest of luck that Burgoyne, himself, survived, having had rifle balls shot through his clothing). Murphy is also thought to have killed Service, the Loyalist and Seth's Henry, the Schoharie chieftain who attempted to return after the war. It is thought that he was killed, as he disappeared soon after returning. Ellerson claimed to have shot and killed the leader of the party of Indians who pursued him on his great race for life. The corpse of the Loyalist Leek shot near Dead Man's Creek was later found, and because of the instruments found with his person, he was believed to have been a surgeon. Besides the casualties, these men also successfully scouted on their own (Murphy is said to have had a "roving commission," that without any orders or instructions, he was free to wage war on the enemy on "his own hook"), and also participated in some of the most arduous campaigns of the war, from the march to Boston in 1775 to the surrender at Yorktown in 1781. No doubt, the true number of losses upon the enemy is considerably higher than fifty.

In return, the enemy inflicted, as far as we know, 3 casualties on these men—Stevens (killed near Harpersfield, April, 1780), Ellerson (wounded twice on June 27, 1779) and Tufts (wounded October 17, 1780), though some of the men could have been wounded prior to their arrival in Schoharie. There are no documented cases of any ever being taken prisoner.

While the rifle certainly deserves some of the credit for their success, this can be too easily pushed as the major factor. It was the man who carried it that earned most of the credit. While it may seem too easy to praise these men and their deeds, we must remember that unlike today, they lived at a time when a man had to call upon all of his senses, his endurance and woodcraft, and even luck just to survive. If they seem larger than life to many of us today, then perhaps it is because measured by today's standards, they are.

Of these men, in his typically flowery prose, Simms wrote:

> *Among the rifle men who went to Schoharie at this time, were some most daring spirits—men whose names should live forever on her fairy mountains and in her green valleys. We do not believe it necessary, although it is a fact too generally conceded, that glittering epaulets are indispensable in forming a hero. Of the brave soldiers sent to aid the Schoharie settlers in their defense, and guard from savage cruelties the unprotected mother and helpless orphan, all of whose names I would gladly chronicle could I collect them—were Lieut. Thomas Boyd ..., Timothy Murphy, David Ellerson, William Leek, William Lloyd, a sergeant, John Wilbur, Zachariah Tufts, Joseph Evans, Felix Hoever, Elijah Hendricks, John Garsaway, a very large man, and Derrick Haggidorn.*

Simms also mentioned the names of the native citizens, mainly rangers, who stood out from the others, men like Jacob and Cornelius Van Dyke, Jacob Enders, Bartholomew C. Vrooman, Peter Van Slyck, Nicholas Slaughter, "Yockam" Folluck, Joackam Van Valkenberg, Jacob Becker, Henry Hager, and Thomas Eckerson. Undoubtedly there were others whose deeds of daring were never recorded and have been long since forgotten.

A history of men like these, and the rifle corps in general, is more than a history of a group of soldiers or a particular military regiment. It is the history of the frontier movement: thousands of frontiersmen, like the handful of men described here, their friends and associates, their offspring and their neighbor's offspring, who had preceded them, lived during their time, and were yet unborn, who rolled the frontier back from the Alleghenies clear to the Pacific coast.

Appendices

Appendice One
Captain Jacob Hager (1734-1819)

Jacob Hager, who would become one of the best known militia officers in the Schoharie region, evidently spent his boyhood at the German Flats in the Mohawk Valley until his father, Hendrick, purchased 78.5 acres of land in the Breakabean area. Here, Jacob, his father, his mother, Gertrude, and four brothers, Joseph, Peter, John and David settled in 1751.

Hendrick served in the French and Indian War, as did Jacob, as a lieutenant under a Captain Sternberg. During the war Hager evidently became known to Joseph Brant.

On October 20, 1775, the 15th Regiment of Albany County was formed by order of General Schuyler and Hager became captain of company number 2. At times this company served at Johnstown, Albany, Fort Edward and Fort Schuyler (Stanwix). Hager participated, along with a party of Schoharie militia, in the Battle of Bemis Heights near Saratoga in the fall of 1777.

Not long after, another company was added, making four in the regiment. According to the Militia Act of New York, all males between the ages of 16 and 60 were required to enroll. The officers from captain on down were chosen by the men of each company. Hager was evidently a popular, as well as efficient leader. Each militiaman was required to furnish himself with a gun, bayonet, sword or tomahawk and ammunition among other necessaries. At his home, he was expected to keep one pound of powder and 3 pounds of balls.

As late as the summer of 1777, no fortifications existed in Schoharie, though four night watches were in effect. Captain Hager's watch consisted of six men at Hendricks' house.

During the familiar three-pronged campaign to invade New York in 1777, a lesser known fourth branch, consisting of 125 Loyalists and Indians under MacDonald and Chrysler began burning and destroying property, including that of Colonel Peter Vroman. Captain Hager, with some of the militia, was barricaded at the Becker house (later fortified, and called the Middle Fort). At this time a large portion of the valley was burned, a time when most of the settlers were still leaning towards the crown. However, Colonel John Harper, with cavalry and rangers, defeated and dispersed the enemy at the Battle of the "Flockey." In this first battle waged in the valley, all of the Hager family were present.[213]

Afterwards three forts were built around the strongest buildings in the area: the stone church, the Becker house and Johannes Feeck's frame dwelling. Hager commanded at the Feeck House, called the "Upper Fort," which was the best fortified and commanded the Old Indian trail to the south which was the most likely spot for the invasion.

In 1779, Captain Hager gained intelligence that Joseph Brant would soon arrive at a destination somewhere on the Delaware River. Hager and about 50 men marched to that area some 30 or 40 miles from Schoharie. They waited in ambush from that afternoon until 10 or 11 a.m. the following morning, when, believing Brant must have taken a different route, returned to Schoharie. According to a Loyalist, less than an hour later Brant and 150 followers arrived where the Americans had been concealed. When informed, the enemy prepared to pursue them until Brant was told the patriot leader was Hager. Brant, who had known Hager in the previous war and respected his courage, desisted, and abandoned the pursuit.

On August 9, 1780, Hager dispatched a scouting party composed of William Leek, Hoever and Winnie in which Leek, contrary to orders, fired at and killed a Tory. Hager's reaction to Leek's disobedience was not recorded, but as the alarm could not be given in time, several men, women, and children were killed and others captured including Henry Hager, nearly 80 years old at the time. He was held captive for eleven months until he was exchanged. While Leek and Joseph Evans seem to have operated under Hager out of the Upper Fort, it was not until November 1, 1780, that most of the other riflemen enlisted in his company. Perhaps they were attracted to Jacob's reputation as a formidable soldier. However, it should be understood that though these men acted as scouts or rangers, Hager's company, as a whole, was a regular militia unit. Men from all four companies often were detached on scouts, as it was the only way to cover the immense area. And even then, the enemy raiders often slipped through undetected. The riflemen, it would seem, were also expected to attend the morning roll calls, when not on a scout.

On October 17, 1780, the large raiding force of Brant and Johnson was seen near the Upper Fort. Captain Hager immediately ordered the alarm gun fired three times, the usual signal for all to get to the forts. Fortunately, Hager was not attacked as he had less than 100 men. However the Middle Fort was invested.

In November, 1781, Adam Chrysler, with a party of 60 or 70 Indians and Loyalists, including the notorious "Seth's Henry," the Schoharie chieftain (who, in a previous raid, left behind a war club, with the bloody record of 75 notches, for 35 scalps and 40 prisoners), attacked the Schoharie in the vicinity of Hager's house. A detachment of rangers, under Tim Murphy, went out to search for the enemy and were fired upon unexpectedly across the Schoharie, in the vicinity of Bouck's Island, near Panther Mountain. In the blast of nearly 70 muskets, only one man, Derrick Haggidorn, was killed. After exchanging fire for some time, the outnumbered rangers retired to the fort. Captain Hager sallied out with 15 or 20 rangers and a company of eastern troops under Captain Hale. That night they encamped beneath a grove of pine trees, in extreme cold, before resuming the pursuit the next day. When ascending the mountains, following the usual route of the invaders, the men finally arrived near Lake Utsayantha on the border of the present town of Jefferson where the enemy fired on them from ambush. Hager commanded Hale, who was marching with his men in the rear, to flank to the right, in an effort to bring the enemy between his command and the lake. Panic must have seized Hale as he turned about and, followed by his men, retreated in double-quick time. Brant took the initiative and advanced on Hager's rangers, now outnumbered some three to one. Hager maneuvered his men to lose only one killed and a few wounded. In the meantime, with Murphy by his side, Hager ran and overtook Hale some 500 yards distant. With firelocks poised to kill, Hager is quoted as thundering, "Run another step and you are a dead man!" This halted the fight, and Hager, attempting to reform and return to the scene of action, was reinforced by Colonel Vroman with some troops. But valuable time had been lost and the enemy departed. The pursuit that followed failed to engage the enemy, and the Americans retreated without further loss to the settlements.

A few more raids occurred in 1782, along with the deaths and destruction that inevitably went hand in hand with them, until, after seven years of war, peace finally returned to the desolated valley. Not until the close of the war did Hager lay down his sword and return, permanently, to the remains of his farm between Breakabean and Blenheim (near present-day Route 30). Captain Hager died on August 21, 1819, at the age of 85 years and is buried at the site of his farm.[214]

The distinctly American dress of the 18th century ranger or frontiersman was widely commented on and set him apart from all of his other contemporaries.

"...Throughout all this country, and in every back settlement in America, the roads and paths are first marked out by blazes on the trees, cut alternately on each side of the way, every thirty or forty yards...The convenience and simplicity of this mode has rendered it universal throughout the whole back country.

"It became the more readily adopted, as all who travel beyond the roads and beaten tracks, always have tomahawks in their belts; which, in such situations and circumstances, are more useful than anything, except the rifle-barreled firelocks; both of which all the male inhabitants habituate themselves constantly to carry along with them everywhere.

"Their whole dress is also very singular, and not very materially different from that of the Indians; being a hunting shirt, somewhat resembling a waggoner's frock, ornamented with a great many fringes, tied round the middle with a broad belt, much decorated also, in which is fastened a tomahawk, an instrument that serves every purpose of defense and convenience; being a hammer at one side and a sharp hatchet at the other; the shot bag and powder-horn, carved with a variety of whimsical figures and devices, hang from their necks over one shoulder; and on their heads a flapped hat, of a reddish hue, proceeding from the intensely hot beams of the sun.

"Sometimes they wear leather breeches, made of Indian dressed elk, or deer skins, but more frequently thin trowsers [sic].

"On their legs they have Indian boots, or leggings, made of coarse woolen cloth, that either are wrapped around loosely and tied with garters, or are laced upon the outside, and always come better than half way up the thigh: these are a great defence and preservative, not only against the bite of serpents and poisonous insects, but likewise against the scratches of thorns, briars, scrubby bushes and underwood, with which this whole country is infested and overspread.

"On their feet they sometimes wear pumps of their own manufacture, but generally Indian moccossons [sic], of their own construction also, which are made of strong elk's or buck's skin, dressed soft as for gloves or breeches, drawn to-gether in regular plaits over the toe, and lacing from thence round to the fore part of the middle of the ancle [sic], without a seam in them, yet fitting close to the feet, and are indeed perfectly easy and pliant.

"Thus habited and accoutered, with his rifle upon his shoulder, or in his hand, a back-wood's man is completely equipped for visiting, courtship, travel, hunting or war.

"And according to the number and variety of the fringes on his hunting shirt, and the decorations on his powder-horn, belt and rifle, he estimates his finery, and absolutely conceives himself of equal consequence, more civilized, polite and more elegantly dressed than the most brilliant peer at St. James's in a splendid and expensive birthday suit, of the first fashion and taste, and most costly materials.

"Their hunting, or rifle shirts, they have also died [sic] in variety of colours, some yellow, others red, some brown and many wear them quite white.

"Such sentiments as those I have just exposed to notice, are neither so ridiculous nor surprising, when the circum-stances are considered with due attention, that prompt the back-wood's American to such a train of thinking, and in which light it is that he feels his own consequence, for he finds all his resources in himself.

"Thus attired and accoutered, as already described, set him in the midst of a boundless forest, a thousand miles from an inhabitant, he is by no means at a loss, nor in the smallest degree dismayed.

"With his rifle he procures his subsistence; with his toma-hawk he erects his shelter, his wigwam, his house or whatever habitation he may chuse [sic] to reside in; he drinks at the crystal spring, or the nearest brook; his wants are all easily sup-plied, he is contented, he is happy. For felicity, beyond a doubt, consists, in a great measure in the attainment and grati-fication of our desires, and the accomplishment of the utmost bounds of our wishes.

"This digression, which I thought necessary to impress an idea of the singular appearance and sentiments of these men, for that reason, I am hopeful, will be excused; and for which, i flatter myself, this will be deemed a sufficient apology."

J. F. D. Smyth, *Tour in the United States of America,* 1784.

"The principle distinction between us, was in our dialects, our arms and our dress. Each man of the three companies bore a rifle-barreled gun, a tomahawk, or small axe, and a long knife, usually called a 'scalping knife,' which served for all purposes, in the woods. His under-dress, by no means in a military style, was covered by a deep ash-colored hunting shirt, leggins and moccasins, if the latter could be procured. It was the silly fashion of those times for the riflemen to ape the manner of savages...

"My wardrobe was scanty and light. It consisted of a roundabout jacket of woolen, a pair of half-worn buckskin breeches, two pairs of woolen stockings (bought at Newbury-port), a hat with a feather, a hunting shirt, leggins, a pair of mockasins [sic], a pair of tolerably good shoes, which had been closely hoarded...

John Joseph Henry
An Accurate and Interesting Account of the Hardships and Sufferings of That Band of Heroes, Who Traversed Thru The Wilderness in the Campaign Against Quebec in 1775, 1812

Appendice Two
Some New Research On Clothing

Doing some research I have come across various details of the dress of riflemen which I thought might be useful to share with those interested.

In the pension account of George Roush, he discusses the clothing of his unit, which was Capt. Samuel Brady's Company (evidently of the 8th Pennsylvania), who operated as scouts out of Fort Pitt. Roush told his applicant writer, "that in obedience of the order of his said Captain Brady, he proceeded to tan his thighs and legs with wild cherry and white oak bark and to equip himself after the following manner, to wit, a breechcloth, leather leggins, moccasins, and a cap made out of a raccoon skin, with the feathers of a hawk, painted red, fastened to the top of the cap. Declarent was then painted after the manner of an Indian warrior. His face was painted red, with three black stripes across his cheeks, which was a signification of war. Declarant states that Captain Brady's company was about sixty-four in number, all painted after the manner aforesaid." Brady became a legendary figure on the Pennsylvania frontier, one of the seemingly countless natural born leaders from the backwoods. He was from Northumberland County – the neighborhood of our own Murphy and Leek. Interestingly, if we believe Roush, his unit was rather successful, on one occasion he and 114 men attacked an Indian camp and killed five (including a squaw). On the way back they were attacked by about 44 Indians. Roush claims only six or seven rounds were fired but 24 Indians were killed and six were wounded. Another time 14 of the rangers espied five Indians crossing the Allegheny River on a raft, fired one volley and killed them all. Roush declared he was involved in seven other skirmishes.

Roush's descriptions check out with those of Moses Van Campen (like Brady he was from Northumberland) who stated several times to his biographer that he and his men often went out on scout dressed entirely in the Indian manner, even to the point of staining their skin to the darker hue of the Indian. Roush's description is invaluable because it tells us how this was done and how the warpaint was applied. Van Campen was so successful in his disguise that on occasion he and his men would fall in with Tories and lead them into traps. When on other duties Van Campen donned his uniform of "bottle green" with red facings, and a hat turned up on one side. Roush also described Brady, a rifle officer, wearing a "French capa coat made of fine sky blue cloth." A capa coat must have been a sort of blanket coat. In *Timothy Murphy, the Benefactor of Schoharie,* by William Sigsby, the author was told of many of Murphy's adventures by his children and others who knew him, and it was frequently stated that he often went out on scout dressed and painted as an Indian. Sigsby claimed that on one such scout, Murphy was pursued by several Indians, killed five or six, and skinned the legs of his last victim, from the hips down, and used the raw hides as leggins.

In *The Public Papers of Gov. George Clinton*, there are a few references to the bedraggled state of the rifle corps stationed in Schoharie in 1778-1779. In vol. 3, pp. 588-590, we find that "118 shirts, 124 shoes, 118 overalls, 29 blankets, 30 napsacks, 60 canteens, and 80 hunting shirts" were wanting in the rifle corps. An on p. 595 we find that "The Rifle men have hardly a Shoe" and they "could not be suppl'd with a single Article." This was in July, 1778, yet during the previous December, just prior to the horrible encampment at Valley Forge, most of the rifle corps were barefoot. Did they actually survive that winter and the campaigning of 1778 without shoes? Throughout that fall in Schoharie, no supplies came in, yet we know of the destruction of the Tories Smith and Service, and the forced march and sacking of Unadilla and Onoquaga, as well as constant scouting. At Unadilla-Onoquaga the men were "Almost bairfooted and Naked." (Clinton Papers, Vol. 4, p. 104). Washington himself finally came to their aid. On Oct 17, 1778, he ordered "80 suits of Uniform, a proportion of shirts and Stockings and 50 blankets and fifty pairs of shoes" for the riflemen in Schoharie, to be drawn from the stores at Springfield. Even on January 25, 1779, Washington was unsure if these articles had reached the men. (*Writings of Washington*, vol. 13, p. 98, p. 96-97, p. 292. Vol. 14, p. 43.) What were "suits of Uniform"? My guess is regimentals, if they ever received them at all.

The record of the rifle corps during this period – constant scouting, Undailla-Oquaga, Onondaga, Sullivan's Expedition, etc., loom all the more remarkable considering their miserable condition.

Dress, Equipage and Firearms
of American Rifle Officers

American "rifle dress" was the result of direct influence of exposure to Indian cultures, as well as some adaptation of traditional European work clothes. While the practicality of moccasins, leggings, breechclouts and the aesthetic values of quillwork, beadwork, flaps and fringes were adopted by the frontiersmen, European or white dress is evident in hunting shirts (which probably developed from the pullover smock or "overshirt" of the European farm laborer), plain white or checked shirts, waistcoats, neckerchiefs, felt hats, breeches, trousers, hard shoes, etc.

Researching the clothing of rifle officers is especially difficult because we are only dealing with a few hundred men who served with the Continental army at any one time. However, indications are that the full scope of clothing worn is extremely wide – everything, in fact, from full Indian dress to full officer's dress. Few officers deserted so we have no deserter descriptions to fall back on. Among the paintings and contemporary descriptions I have been able to find are the following:

• John Joseph Henry, in his narrative, *Campaign Against Quebec,* Lancaster, 1812, of which he was a participant, described Daniel Morgan's appearance, at the time (1775) a captain, during the grueling march through the wilderness of Maine. "His thighs, which were exposed to view, appeared to have been lacerated by the thorns and bushes" because "He wore leggins and a cloth in the Indian style." Henry also stated that they wore white blanket coats and fur caps during the siege and assault on Quebec.

• John Trumbull recalled the dress of Morgan and his officers during the siege of Boston in 1775. "You expressed apprehension that the rifle dress of General Morgan* may be mistaken hereafter for a waggoner's frock which he, perhaps, wore when on the expedition with General Braddock; there is no more resemblance between the two dresses, than between a cloak and coat; the waggoner's frock was intended, as the present cartman's, to cover and protect their other clothes, and is merely a long coarse shirt reaching below the knee; the dress of the Virginia rifle-men who came to Cambridge in 1775 (among whom was Morgan) was an elegant loose dress reaching to the middle of the thigh, ornamented with fringes in various parts and meeting the pantaloons of the same material and color, fringed and ornamented in corresponding style. The officers wore the usual crimson sash over this, and around the waist, the straps, belts, etc. were black, forming in my opinion, a very picturesque and elegant as well as useful dress. It cost a trifle; the soldier could wash it at any brook he passed; however worn and ragged and dirty his other clothing might be, when this was thrown over it, he was in elegant uniform." From Copeland, Peter, *Working Dress in Colonial America.* In the early stages of the war, General Washington was much enamored of the hunting shirt as it was a "utilitarion" garment, however as the war progressed the regimental coat became much more common. Less practical, it was considered more military-like in an American army attempting to emulate the professional armies of Europe. By early 1778, General Anthony Wayne, a stickler for uniforms, had reduced his Pennsylvania Brigade to less than one-seventh hunting shirts, the rest in regimentals. In that same year a regular line officer showed up on parade dressed in his hunting shirt when it was well known he possessed a regimental coat. The case was brought up through the chain of command to Washington himself, who, while trying to fight the world's greatest empire, was much concerned about this breach of discipline! Instead of a court-martial, this officer was only publicly rebuked as an example. This illustrates how militarized the thinking in the army was becoming. From the *Writings of Washington*, Vol. 13.

• Evidence would indicate that rifle officers, like officers of any other regiment, were interested in achieving a military-like bearing. After the Battle of Princeton on January 3, 1777, an artillery sergeant "... looked round the room, and saw an officer's coat – I went to it and found it a new one; the paper never taken off the buttons, was plated or solid silver, I could not determine which, lined with white satin..." Later, "The coat I sold to an officer of an rifle regiment (the uniform answered to his description but for the buttons; it belonged to the 40th Regiment, faced with white) for 18 dollars. That regiment all the commissioned officers wore red coats, face with white..." What regiment was this? The First Regiment of the Continental line, previously Thompson's Rifle Battalion, had been ordered to change their clothing to brown regimental coats, but General Wayne complained that they were still clad in hunting shirts and armed with rifles in the Spring of 1777. From Katcher, Philip, *Military Dress in North America*. In his painting of the assault on Quebec, the artist John Trumbull depicted Colonel William Thompson in blue regimentals, waistcoat, stock, bi-corn, etc., along with Captain William Hendricks who was clad in a brown hunting shirt and matching trousers. Trumbull's paintings were done in the 1780s, 1790s and early 1800s, and his figures are probably more stylistic than actual portraits of people he never met.

• Moses Van Campen was a militia rifle officer and states many times quite clearly that he and his men were armed with rifles. When he was an old man, he recited his adventures to J. Niles Hubbard, who published *The Life and*

Adventures of Major Moses Van Campen in 1842. Van Campen recalled one episode in which he came close to death, in a way in which he remembered his clothing at the time. In 1782, when he was a prisoner of the Senecas, an Indian told him he had seen him before, and was prepared to kill him but desisted when he discovered Van Campen's party was stronger than he thought. The Indian then described what Van Campen was wearing to confirm what he said was true. He had been on a journey of some military business and was thus dressed in his uniform as a lieutenant in Captain Robinson's Rangers of Northumberland County. The Indian said he "wore a suit of bottle green turned up with red" and a "large cap with a cockade, part white, part black, and a feather in the top." Van Campen described the duty of rangers on scouts and the clothing they wore on those occasions. One time a scout consisting of five men, one of whom was a captain and two others lieutenants who "assumed the Indian dress and color," actually painting their skins the hue of the Indians', complete with war paint. Clothing on such scouts consisted of hunting shirts, leggings, breechclouts and moccasins, which Van Campen referred to repeatedly.

• Trumbull's famous painting of Burgoyne's surrender at Saratoga depicts Col. Daniel Morgan, among others dressed in their various uniforms. Morgan wears a fine linen hunting shirt (with a cape in one version, without in another), evidently a pullover with matching trousers. A sash is tied about his waist and a black leather strap crosses one shoulder. Beneath his hunting shirt can be seen a ruffled shirt and a buff-colored waistcoat. Also evident is a black stock, plain leather moccasins, and he leans on a sword. His hair appears to be powdered. A painting by 19th-century artist Alonzo Chappel also shows Morgan in similar dress.

• Another painting by Trumbull, depicting the surrender of the Germans at Trenton, shows an officer on the left side, dressed in typical rifle clothes. (He actually was a colonel in a Virginia regiment.) He wears a wraparound style hunting shirt of what appears to be fine linen, a buff waistcoat, ruffled shirt, black stock, cloth breeches, stockings, half gaiters and shoes. His hair is not powdered and is tied back in the usual style. He leans on his sword. A crimson sash is evident.

• A painting by De Verger, done during the war, illustrates a rifleman, possibly an officer, wearing shoes, overalls of a greyish hue, a white hunting shirt with a cape, black stock and a low crowned wide-brimmed hat of greenish tint topped off with feathers. His rather large hunting bag has a wide leather strap of a brown color. His rifle has a sling attached.

• A sketch by Du Simitiere for the Great Seal of the United States shows a rifleman who appears to be an officer. This man wears shoes, trousers and hunting shirt of cloth or deerskin, trimmed with fur, a stock and fur cap with a mobile visor folded back. The style of coat which falls almost to the knee was seen for several decades on the frontier and is held closed with a sash. It may be of wool, seems to be fitted at the shoulder, and has tight sleeves. A collar is evident and the fur trim has been attached at the shoulder, cuff and bottom of the body. The matching trousers have a fur trim at the cuff. His hair is tied back. A pouch and horn can be seen and the rifle appears to be a transitional piece. Daniel Boone was painted by Alonzo Chappel in a similar coat.

Firearms

As for firearms of rifle officers, the evidence seems to indicate two important things – officers used longarms and these seem to have been rifles. Some have stated that among the men in Morgan's Rifle corps (1777-1779) were soldiers recruited from line units armed with muskets. I have been unable to document that, but it does not mean it is not possible. This supposition seems to be based on the fact that at various times detachments of light infantry were ordered to serve as a back-up to Morgan's Riflemen, and while under Morgan's command, were never an actual part of his regiment. While the men of this corps were chosen from many regiments, they all seem to have been armed with rifles, they were all picked for their marksmanship, and were referred to that way. In regular units officers often did not use a musket as they were expected to be too busy issuing orders during battle to spend time loading and firing their own weapons. However, among ranger and rifle-type units, this seems never to have been the case. The men were trained to act and fire pretty much on their own, thus leaving the officers free to do likewise. Just prior to the attack on King's Mountain in 1780, Colonel John Sevier told his militia riflemen not to expect orders, that each man knew his duty, and was his own officer. This seems to be true of most rifle regiments as well as some Loyalist units, such as Butler's Rangers. There is evidence of rifle officers using their own weapons in combat:

- Capt. David Harris wrote to Gen. Edward Hand on August 13, 1777, in which he mentioned an exploit of Capt. James Parr of Morgan's Rifle Corps. "Captain Parr has killed three or four men himself this summer. His expressions at the Death of one I shall ever remember. Major Miller had the Command of a Detachment, and had a skirmish at very close shot with a party of Highlanders. One of them being quite open, he motioned to Capt. Parr to kill him, which he did in a thrice, and, as he was falling, Parr said: 'I say, by God, Sawny, I am in you.' I assure Parr's bravery on every occasion does him great Honour." from *Northumberland County in the American Revolution*, Northumberland County Historical Society, 1976.

- Capt. Gabriel Long of Morgan's Rifle Corps shot and killed a Capt. Charles Smith, a Loyalist, in the opening shot of an ambush on the Schoharie River in early August, 1778. "Capt. Long of the Riffle men fired at and shot Smith through the head," said one account of August 9, 1778, and another that "Capt. Long fell in with them, Kill'd Smith & Brought in his Scalp," dated August 13. From *The Public Papers of George Clinton*, Vol. III.

• John Henry, in his narrative of the march to Quebec, mentioned several officers using rifles. He wrote, "At the distance, perhaps, of one hundred and fifty yards, a shooting-match took place, and believe me, the balls of Morgan, Simpson, Humphreys and others, played around, and within a few inches of his head." All of these men were rifle officers, of Morgan's, Hendricks' and Smith's Companies. Henry also wrote, "Hendricks, when aiming his rifle at some prominent person, died by a straggling ball..." From Henry, John, *Campaign Against Quebec*, Lancaster, 1812.

• Moses Van Campen frequently mentioned his use of the rifle. He was promoted to lieutenant of a militia ranger unit, and when choosing men for a scout or a daring mission would hold up a block of wood and only those who could hit the target the closest would be chosen. Van Campen did not usually go far before finding the required number of marksmen. From Hubbard's *Life and Adventures of Moses Van Campen*. 1842.

Thus it would seem that the officers, like the men, used rifles, with no indications whatsoever of muskets, carbines, trade guns or even halberds, pikes or spontoons being used, as in other regiments. However, the type of clothing worn varied greatly. In 1775, we might have seen an officer of Thompson's Rifle Battalion in a hunting shirt with matching trousers, or perhaps breechclout and leggins, and definitely a rifle. It is possible he would have been wearing some civilian-type clothing. Later in the war we might have found a rifle officer in a complete military uniform, but still with a rifle. On the other hand, a frontier ranger officer could be found to be dressed entirely in the Indian fashion during the same period.

Appendice Three
Monuments Erected to the Memory of the Riflemen

Even into our own century, the names of these men and their deeds of daring have not been forgotten. The following is a list of all the monuments and plaques that I know of.

Saratoga Battlefield – a marker with the following inscription:
THE SHOT THAT KILLED GEN. FRASER OCT. 7, 1777 WAS FIRED FROM NEAR HERE BY TIMOTHY MURPHY OF MORGAN'S RIFLEMEN. By the state of New York in 1929. In that year Gov. Franklin Roosevelt spoke on the site and paid tribute to Murphy's alleged shot. Also a monument erected by the "Ancient Order of Hibernians" in 1913, carries this inscription: "...TO THE MEMORY OF TIMOTHY MURPHY, CELEBRATED MARKSMAN OF COLONEL MORGAN'S RIFLE CORPS, WHOSE UNERRING AIM TURNED THE TIDE OF BATTLE BY THE DEATH OF THE BRITISH GENERAL FRASER ON OCTOBER 7, 1777, THEREBY ADDING TO THE WORLD'S HISTORY ONE OF ITS DECISIVE BATTLES. IN THIS MONUMENT IS COMMEMORATED HEROIC DEEDS OF HUNDREDS OF OTHER SOLDIERS OF IRISH BLOOD WHO LAID DOWN THEIR LIVES ON THIS BLOODY FIELD THAT THE UNION OF STATES MIGHT BE TRIUMPHANT."

Schoharie County – several other markers to Tim Murphy are: a rest stop on Rte 30, near Bouck's Island, proclaiming that road the "Timothy Murphy Trail," and across the road and a short distance to the north is a plaque put on the site of his first house with Peggy Feeck, both of these erected by the state. Near by is the beautiful site of the "Upper Fort."

After Murphy's marriage to his second wife, Mary Robertson, he lived for five years at South Worcester, where a marker erected by the State Education Department bears the following inscription: "MURPHY HOME, TIMOTHY MURPHY, FAMOUS REVOLUTIONARY SOLDIER LIVED ON THIS FARM, 1812-1817."

Murphy, who died in 1818, was buried in the Feeck family plot, but in 1872 his remains were removed to the Middleburgh cemetery, where, lying beside Peggy, his spirit commands a fine view of the valley. His tombstone in inscribed "Timothy Murphy died June 27, 1818 aged 67 years," followed by a glorious poem, too long to repeat here. Next to his grave is an impressive granite and bronze monument to Murphy in which a bas relief impression of him in inaccurate clothing is depicted. The inscription reads: "TO THE MEMORY OF TIMOTHY MURPHY, PATRIOT, SOLDER, SCOUT, CITIZEN, WHO SERVED IN MORGAN'S RIFLE CORPS. FOUGHT AT SARATOGA AND MONMOUTH AND WHOSE BRAVERY REPELLED THE ATTACK OF THE BRITISH AND· THEIR INDIAN ALLIES UPON THE MIDDLE FORT, OCTOBER 17, 1780, AND SAVED THE COLONISTS OF SCHOHARIE VALLEY." It was erected in 1910.

Old Stone Fort – Just to the left of the entrance to the church is a plaque to the memory of David Ellerson, "MEMORIAL TO .DAVID ELLERSON, 1749-1838, SCHOHARIE COUNTY REVOLUTIONARY HERO, PATRIOT, SOLDIER, SCOUT, MEMBER OF MORGAN'S RIFLE CORPS. SERVED AT TRENTON, MONMOUTH, SARATOGA AND IN SULLIVAN'S CAMPAIGN. ONE OF THE CAPTORS OF SERVICE THE TORY. ESPECIALLY DISTINGUISHED FOR BRAVERY ON SCOUT DUTY IN

SCHOHARIE VALLEY. FOUGHT AT BATTLE OF MIDDLE FORT, AGAINST COL. JOHNSON AND CHIEF BRANT." It was erected in 1929. David was buried in Flat Creek cemetery near Gilboa, but his family was too poor to erect a tombstone. A devoted great-grandson, however, inscribed on a slab of sandstone, crudely but lovingly, "DAVID ELLERSON, THE HERO OF THE REVOLUTION" and so it stood until a more appropriate monument was erected by the American Legion Society. This simple tombstone is on display in the Old Stone Fort.

Flat Creek Cemetery – in the northwest corner is the impressive monument mentioned above. On it is Ellerson's name and a list of a few of the battles he was in. A small American flag graces the plot.

Middleburgh, NY – In Memorial Park on Main Street is a large stone monument dedicated to the defenders of the Middle Fort. It is faced with three bronze plaques, one a list of the men of the Third Co., 15th Reg't of Albany County, another dedicated to four veterans buried there (one of whom is Jacob Van Dyke, said to be a local rifleman), and the third to the defenders of the fort.

Among some of the more outstanding defenders of the Middle Fort were listed by name as "MORGAN'S RIFLEMEN AND RANGERS, TIM MURPHY, DAVID ELLERSON, JOHN WILBUR, SGT. WILLIAM LLOYD, PHILIP HOEVER, WILLIAM LEEK, JOACHIM FOLLUCK, RICHARD HANSON, ZACHARIAH TUFTS." Among the wounded was Tufts' name engraved a second time. Listed among the women defenders was the following: SUSANNAH VROOMAN, WHO BROUGHT A LIVE COAL FOR THE OFFICER OF ARTILLERY, LIVINGSTON, FOR THE

PURPOSE OF FIRING A GUN." Susannah later married Philip Hoever. Erected in 1934.

Genesee Valley – at a location near Groveland, NY, there is a monument to the men who were ambushed there under Lt. Thomas Boyd on September 13, 1779. Among those listed is Tim Murphy who escaped along with several of his comrades, but most of this scout was massacred on the site. Boyd had been stationed in Schoharie for the past year. He and another rifleman, Pvt. Michael Parker were captured and later that day tortured to death by the Indians at a site near modern Leicester, just off Rte. 39-20A, where there is a monument to them. At Mount Hope Cemetery, another monument marks the spot where Boyd's remains as well as the remains of a dozen or more killed with him were reinterred in 1841. This event was marked by a large ceremony in which two elderly riflemen, Moses Van Campen and John Salmon (who had escaped the ambush) were guest speakers. This cemetery is located in Rochester.

Natural Landmarks Named for the Men

"Murphy Hill" – located between Cooperstown and Middlefield, so called because it was in an area Murphy often scouted around.

"Murphy Mountain" – located near Walton in Delaware County, another location he and his comrades scouted over.

"Dead Man's Creek" – a small stream that enters the Schoharie a few miles below the location of the Upper Fort. Simms actually provides us with two explanations for its name. First, he wrote it was named for the Tory William

Leek shot before the latter ran for his life, and second for a Tory killed by Murphy at Bouck's Island in Nov. 1781. At any rate it was still one of the riflemen who did the act that gave it its name, a name it still holds.

"Torture Tree" – a yet living memento of the riflemen from Schoharie, an ancient oak tree said to be the one Boyd and Parker were tied to before being hacked to death.

Behind Ellerson's house, still standing near Gilboa, NY, is an old tree that at one time was a target for riflemen. This target is now about 15 or 20 feet above the ground and is identified as such by the scars on it and rifle caliber balls dug out of it. Imagine – a living thing once the private property of Ellerson, an object once used as a target by, perhaps, his sons, or even the other riflemen!

Homes of the Men

As mentioned above, Ellerson's home is yet standing near Gilboa. He and Sarah Beagraft probably moved into it around 1785 and it was situated on the 600-acre tract he received for his services in the war. It is a small one-story frame dwelling.

Captain Hager's farmhouse, being restored, is located near Blenheim, and is beautifully situated on the Schoharie River. This was the site of a shoot in 1799, in which several of the men participated. Nearby is the Hager family burial plot, where a monument has been erected to the captain. So far I have found no less than 16 monuments, tombstones or plaques dealing with the riflemen or their associates; 5 natural landmarks (2 still living); and 2 existing homes.

Muster Roll Of The Rifle Corps In 1779

Originally commanded by Colonel Daniel Morgan from the spring of 1777 until July of 1778, when he relinquished command upon giving command to the 7th Virginia. Six of the eight companies were broken up, the men returned to their former units. Only the companies of Captains Parr and Long remained, until they, too, were dissolved at West Point in November, 1779.

What follows is a listing of the men of the two remaining companies based upon payrolls taken in 1779.

*denotes those who returned to the Schoharie region after the expiration of their enlistments

OFFICERS

James Parr, Major
John Coleman, Adjutant
Henry Henly, Quartermaster
Benjamin Ashby, Paymaster
Daniel Shute, Surgeon
Michael Simpson, Captain
Gabriel Long, Captain (resigned May 13, 1779)
Philip Slaughter, Captain Lieutenant Nov. 1, 1778; Captain
    May 13, 1779
Thomas Boyd, Lieutenant
William Stephens (Stevens) Lieutenant
Elijah Evans, Lieutenant
Benjamin Ashby, Lieutenant
Reuben Long, Ensign; Lieutenant May 10, 17??
John Howe, Sergeant Major

"A Pay Roll of Captn. Simpson's Company of Detached Rifle Men for the Month of August 1779."

Michael Simpson, Captn.
Thomas Boyd, Lt. (tortured to death, September 13, 1779)
Wm. Stephens, Lt. * (active on the Unadilla-Onoquaga campaign in 1778; apparently killed near Harpersfield, NY, in April, 1780.)
Stephen Sims, Sergt.
Jonathan Armstrong, Sergt.
Jonathan McMahon, Sergt.
Jonathon Watson, Sergt.
Benjamin Custard, Sergt.
John Ray, Corpl.
Thomas Benston, Corpl.
John Kelly, Corpl.
John Ryan, Corpl.
Michael Parker, Private (tortured to death, Sept. 13, 1779)
Albert Weaver
William Linn
William Kerr
Anthony Granad
Nichs Chocer
Alexander Thompson
Peter Condon
David Davis
James Elliot
Patrick McCaw
Felix Hoover (Hoever)*
Philip Potter
John Yost (survived ambuscade near Genesee, Sept. 13, 1779)

John Solomon (Salmon; survived ambuscade near Genesee;
    still alive in Avon, NY, in 1840)
John Curry
Samuel Poarter
James Hambelton
Edward Lee
John Casper
Edward Huselen
Robert Shepherd
Timothy Murphy (legendary Indian fighter, reputed to have
    killed over 40 of the enemy)*
Isaac Heselton
James Crage
John Erwin
Jedh (Zachariah) Tufts*
William Rabb
John McCreery
John McKenny (McKenzie; was a spy sent into Unadilla in
    August, 1778)
John Williber (Wilbur)*
Joseph King
Robert McDonol
Daniel Hidden
William English
John Tidd (survived march to Quebec in 1775-1776)
Daniel McMullen
Benjamin Wheeler

"Payroll of the late Capt. Gabriel Long's Company of De-
tach'd Rifle Men formerly commanded by Colo. Daniel Morgan for the month of July 1779."

Elijah Evans, Lt. (commanded detachment of riflemen on
    the Onondaga Campaign, April, 1779)
Benjamin Ashby, Lt.

Reuben Long, Ensign
John Howe, Sergeant (discharged July 25)
Nicholas Long, Sergeant (discharged Aug 1)
Elias Tolland, Sergeant
Thomas Coleman, Sergeant (discharged Aug. 1)
Joseph Evans, Sergeant*
Jeremiah Samuel, Sergeant
Samuel Burks, Sergeant
Smith Kent, Sergeant
Rowley Jacobs, Corporal
John Gazaway (Garsaway), Corporal
William Sudeth, Corporal (discharged July 23)
Vincent Howell, Corporal (discharged July 23)
Elijah Hendricks, Corporal
Duncan McDonald, Corporal
William Lloyd (Loyd), Private
Jacob Smith
James Wilson
James Harris
Jesse Wilhite
Patrick Howracan (discharged Aug. 1)
Henry Holdaway (discharged Aug. 1)
Charles Morgan
Daniel Grant (discharged Aug. 1)
Mack Robinson
John Straughan (discharged July 24)
John Grant (discharged Aug. 1)
Thomas Dermott
John Colman (Coleman; discharged Aug. 1)
John McJohnson (discharged Aug. 1)
Moses Spencer
Samuel Davis (discharged Aug. 1)
John Hopewell
Benjamin McKnight
William Castle

Reuben Long, Private
Thomas Wright
David Ellison (Allison, Elerson, Ellerson; famous ranger of
    Schoharie; related to Simms account of his and his com-
    rades' exploits)
Christopher Kooney
Joseph Vance
John Smith (discharged Aug. 1)
John Lyon
William Jacobs
Daniel Davidson (Davis)
John Robinson
John Austin
William Hartlett
Samuel Middleton
Richard Roundsiver
James Jiles
John Adams
William Haddle (discharged Aug. 1)
William Darby (discharged Aug. 1)
Andrew Elder
James McGuire
Daniel Dunnegan
Charles Witt
Richard Skeggs

Additions and Corrections:
On June 16, 1779, John Allen, Thomas Burk, Samuel Fal-
ling, and Thomas Davis deserted (evidently when the rifle
corps was ascending the Mohawk River, on its way to Cana-
joharie, to join the troops assembled there under General
Clinton.)
William Leek* was a member of Simpson's company.
Philip Hoever (Hoover)* was a member of the rifle corps.

Riflemen in typical dress preparing for an ambush. These are members of the recreated Captain Hager's Company, 15th Regiment of Albany County, who represent ten riflemen who returned to the Scoharie Valley, enlisted in the militia, and served for the most part as rangers or scouts, making quite a name for themselves. Photo by Gilbert Dabkowski.

Endnotes

[1] For descriptions of the riflemen, their arms, equipment, and clothing, see:
Dillin, Captain John, *The Kentucky Rifle*, Washington, D.C., 1924
Peterson, Harold, *The Book of the Continental Soldier*, Stackpole
Books, Harrisburg, 1968
Neumann, George C., *The History of Weapons of the American Revolution*, NY, 1972

[2] Cook, Frederick. *Journals of the Military Expedition of Major General John Sullivan against the Six Nations of Indians in 1779*. 1887: Auburn, NY. Reprinted 2000, Heritage Books, Inc., Bowie, Maryland. Hereafter cited as *Sullivan's Indian Expedition*

[3] O'Brien, Michael J., *Timothy Murphy, Hero of the Revolution*, NY, 1941, p. 161

[4] Washington to Morgan, August 16, 1777, John C. Fitzpatrick, ed., *Writings of Washington*, IX, p. 71

[5] Verbal discourse with Mr. H. Kels Swan, President of the Daniel Morgan Memorial Foundation, South Bound Brook, NJ, in 1978. Also see Callahan, North, *Daniel Morgan, Ranger of the Revolution*, NY, 1961, p. 149

[6] Higginbotham, Don, *Daniel Morgan, Revolutionary Rifleman*, Chapel Hill, NC, 1961, pp. 79-80

[7] Peterson, *Book of the Continental Soldier*, pp. 43-44. Also see Hangar, Col. George, *Notes to all Sportsmen*, London, 1814

[8] Thompson, Ray, *Washington at Whitemarsh, Prelude to Valley Forge*, Fort Washington, PA, 1974. The three main Morgan biographers, Graham, Higginbotham and Callahan, also cite evidence of the bravery and effectiveness of Morgan's riflemen during this engagement

[9] Simms, Jeptha, *Frontiersmen of New York*, 1883, Vol. 2, pp. 696-697

[10] For a detailed account of the activities of Morgan's Riflemen, see Graham, James, *The Life of General Daniel Morgan*, 1856

[11] As determined from Revolutionary War Pension Files, National Archives

[12] Washington to Stark, July 18, 1778, Fitzpatrick, ed., *Writings of Washington*, Vol. 12, p. 190

[13] Ibid, Washington to Congress, Vol. 12, p. 214

[14] Ibid, Washington to Stark, Vol. 12, p. 284

[15] Ibid, Washington to Congress, Vol. 12, p. 214

[16] Ibid, Washington to Posey, Vol. 12, p. 285

[17] *Public Papers of George Clinton, 1778*, Vol. III, Albany, 1900, pp. 588-590. Hereafter cited as *Clinton Papers*

[18] Ibid, Butler to Clinton, July 29, 1778, Vol. III, p. 595

[19] Ibid, Ten Broeck to Clinton, August 1, 1778, Vol. III, p. 599

[20] Ibid, Major Joseph Becker to Brigadier General Ten Broeck, Vol. III, pp. 594-595

[21] Ibid, Ten Broeck to Clinton, Vol. III, pp. 599-600

[22] Simms, *Frontiersmen*, Vol. II, p. 188

[23] *Clinton Papers*, Butler to Clinton, August 13, 1778, Vol. III, pp. 630-632

[24] Simms, *Frontiersmen*, Vol. 2, p. 186

[25] *Clinton Papers*, John Taylor to Clinton, August 9, 1778, Vol. III, p. 616. Taylor claimed the number of Loyalists was about 25; Simms said about 90

[26] Ibid, Butler to Clinton, Vol. III, p. 631

[27] Ibid

[28] Ibid, p. 632

[29] Ibid, p. 710

[30] Ibid, p. 140

[31] For details of this affair and the depositions of Posey, Long, and Lt. Alexander Ramsey (of the 4th PA) see the *Clinton Papers*, Vol. III, pp. 728-729, 738-740, and Vol. IV, pp. 103-111, 139-141

[32] Ibid, Vol. III, p. 108

[33] Ibid, p. 711

[34] *Minutes of the Commissioners for Detecting and Defeating Conspiracies in the State of New York*, NY 1972, Vol. 1, p. 2

[35] Ibid, p. 245

[36] *Clinton Papers*, Vol. III, pp. 711-712

[37] Ibid, Vol. IV, p. 104

[38] *Sullivan's Indian Expedition*, Captain William Gray, p. 289

[39] See Butler's Journal in the *Clinton Papers*, Vol. IV, p. 223

[40] Ibid, p. 231

[41] O'Brien, Michael J. *Timothy Murphy, Hero of the Revolution*, NY, 1941, p. 45.

[42] *Writings of Washington*, Vol. 13, p. 135

[43] Ibid, p. 98

[44] Ibid, p. 96-97

[45] Ibid, p. 98

[46] Ibid, p. 292

[47] Ibid, p. 43

[48] Ibid, p. 439

[49] Ibid, Vol. 14, p. 43

[50] Ibid, Vol. 14, p. 188

[51] Schoharie County church records (known as Albany County then)

[52] Simms, *Frontiersmen*, Vol. 2, p. 413

[53] Monthly Strength Reports of the Continental Army. John Coleman was adjutant for the rifle corps

[54] *Sullivan's Indian Expedition*, Lt. Erkuries Beatty, p. 16.

[55] Ibid

[56] Clark, Joshua V. H. *Onondaga; Or Reminiscences of Earlier and Later Times*, Syracuse, 1849, Vol. 1, p. 330

[57] Present Syracuse, New York

[58] These towns were situated near the southern shore of Onondaga Lake

[59] Clark, *Onondaga*, p. 331

[60] Ibid

[61] *Sullivan's Indian Expedition*, Lt. Beatty, p. 18

[62] *Sullivan's Indian Expedition*, Thomas Machin, p. 193

[63] *Sullivan's Indian Expedition*, Lt. Beatty, p. 17

[64] Clark, *Onondaga*, p. 332

[65] *Writings of Washington*, Vol. 15, pp. 27, 54

[66] *Sullivan's Indian Expedition*, Lt. Beatty, p. 18

[67] *Writings of Washington*, Vol. 15, p. 306

[68] Ibid, p. 45

[69] Monthly Strength Reports of the Continental Army, June, 1779

[70] Minutes of the Commissioners, Vol. 1, pp. 335, 356, 359-360, 395, 397, 398, 402, 404, 413, 426

[71] O'Brien, *Timothy Murphy*, pp. 47-49

[72] *Sullivan's Indian Expedition*, Lt. Beatty, p. 18

[73] Ibid, p. 19

[74] *The Order Book of Captain Leonard Bleeker, Major of Brigade*, NY, 1865, p. 34

[75] Site of present Cooperstown, NY

[76] *Sullivan's Indian Expedition*, Lt. Beatty, p. 19

[77] *Sullivan's Indian Expedition*. The journals of Beatty, June 27, p. 19; Lt. William McKenary, June 27, p. 199, and Lt. Rudolphus Van Hovenburgh, June 29, p. 276, mention this incident

[78] Simms, *Frontiersmen*, Vol. 2, pp. 301-302

[79] Revolutionary War Pension Files, National Archives, Deposition of David Ellison

[80] Yoackim Van Valkenburgh, who served as a ranger in Schoharie and was killed in action at Lake Utsayantha, November, 1781

[81] *The Order Book of Captain Leonard Bleeker*, pp. 69, 70

[82] Ibid, p. 86

[83] Ibid, p. 97

[84] *Sullivan's Indian Expedition*, Lt. Beatty, p. 22

[85] *The Order Book of Captain Leonard Bleeker*, pp. 101, 104-105

[86] Ibid, p. 107

[87] *Sullivan's Indian Expedition*, Lt. Col. Adam Hubley, p. 128; Rev. Willam Rogers, D.D., p. 263

[88] *The Order Book of Captain Leonard Bleeker*, p. 128

[89] *Sullivan's Indian Expedition*, Lt. Beatty, p. 22

[90] *Sullivan's Indian Expedition*, Lt. Col. Adam Hubley, p. 154

[91] Sigsby, William, *Timothy Murphy, the Benefactor of Schoharie*. 1839, pp. 9-10

[92] *Sullivan's Indian Expedition*, Sgt. Nathaniel Webb, p. 286

[93] *Sullivan's Indian Expedition*, Lt. Col. Adam Hubley, p. 154

[94] Ibid

[95] *Sullivan's Indian Expedition*, Lt. Beatty, p. 27

[96] *Sullivan's Indian Expedition*, Thomas Grant, p. 140

[97] *Sullivan's Indian Expedition*, Lt. John Jenkins, p. 172

[98] *Sullivan's Indian Expedition*, Sgt.Moses Fellows, p. 88

[99] Ibid

[100] *Sullivan's Indian Expedition*, Lt. John Jenkins, p. 172

[101] *Sullivan's Indian Expedition*, Lt. Col. Adam Hubley, p. 157

[102] *Sullivan's Indian Expedition*, Captain John Livermore, p. 186

[103] *Sullivan's Indian Expedition*, Lt. Beatty, p. 28

[104] Ibid, p. 29

[105] *Sullivan's Indian Expedition*, Lt. Col. Adam Hubley, p. 160

[106] Ibid

[107] *Sullivan's Indian Expedition*, Dr. Jabez Campfield, p. 57

[108] *Sullivan's Indian Expedition*, Lt. Beatty, p. 31

[109] See Ibid, the journals of Beatty and Hubley, and General Sullivan's official report, for the best descriptions of this action. The enemy force amounted to about 400 men

[110] *Sullivan's Indian Expedition*, Lt. Col. Adam Hubley, p. 161

[111] That Parker was the other rifleman captured is determined from the journal of Captain John Livermore, Ibid, p. 188

[112] Ibid, Lt. Col. Adam Hubley, p. 161; Lt. Beatty, p. 31

[113] *Sullivan's Indian Expedition*, Thomas Grant, surveyor, p. 142

[114] *Sullivan's Indian Expedition*, Lt. Col. Henry Dearborn, p. 75

[115] O'Brien, *Timothy Murphy, Hero of the Revolution*, p. 58

[116] Letter from Col. John Butler to Lt. Col. Bolton, September 14, 1779, The Sullivan-Clinton Campaign in 1779, Albany, 1929, p. 129. An unsigned letter of September 19, 1779, says essentially the same thing

[117] *Sullivan's Indian Expedition*, Lt. Col. Adam Hubley, pp. 162-163

[118] *Notices of Sullivan's Campaign*, 1842, reprinted 1970, p. 175

[119] Ibid, pp. 37-70, 134

[120] *Sullivan's Indian Expedition*, Dr. Jabez Campfield, p. 57

[121] *Sullivan's Indian Expedition*, Hubley, p. 163

[122] *Sullivan's Indian Expedition*, Thomas Grant, p. 142

[123] Ibid, p. 143

[124] *Sullivan's Indian Expedition*, Sgt. Major George Grant, p. 113

[125] *Sullivan's Indian Expedition*, Thomas Grant, p. 143

[126] *Sullivan's Indian Expedition*, Sgt Major George Grant, p. 113

[127] *Sullivan's Indian Expedition*, Lt William McKendry, p. 206; Lt Rudolphus Van Hovenburgh, p. 283

[128] *General Orders*, Edward Scammel, November 9, 1779

[129] Trevelyan, George, *The American Revolution*, New York, 1909, part III, p. 151

[130] Sparks, Jared, *Memoirs*.

[131] Information on Thomas Posey can be found in his *Memoirs*, written by Jared Sparks, and taken largely from his papers, vol. 19, pp. 363-403; *National Cyclopaedia of American Biography*, vol. XIII, pp. 265-266; and Heitman, *Historical Register of Officers of the Continental Army*, Washington, D.C., 1914, pp. 333-334

[132] Stroh, Oscar, *Thompson's Rifle Battalion*, Harrisburg, 1974

[133] Snyder, Charles F., *Northumberland County in the American Revolution*, Northumberland Historical Society, 1976, p. 34

[134] Boatner, III, Mark, *Encyclopedia of the American Revolution*, p. 603

[135] Snyder, ed., *Northumberland County in the American Revolution*, p. 53

[136] Ibid

[137] Wright, Col. John Womack, *Some Notes on the Continental Army*, Cornwallville, NY, p. 57; Heitman, Francis B., *Historical Register of Officers of the Continental Army*

[138] Heitman, *Historical Register*

[139] Henry, John Joseph, *March to Quebec*, Lancaster, 1812. References to Simpson can be found on pp. 4, 54-60, 62, 65, 68-70, 72, 74-76, 81, 90-91, 94, 105-7, 144, 220-222

[140] Heitman, *Historical Register*, p. 367

[141] Stroh, Oscar, *Thompson's Rifle Battalion*

[142] Henry, *March to Quebec*; references to Boyd can be found on pp. 17-50, 133, 140, 148-162, 172, 192-193, 201-204, 222

[143] Heitman, *Historical Register*, p. 94

[144] Simms, *Frontiersmen*, Vol. II, p. 246

[145] Several journals note this incident, notably that of Lt. Col. Adam Hubley, in *Sullivan's Indian Expedition*, p. 128

[146] Henry, *March to Quebec*, p. 222

[147] Ibid

[148] Tour of Mount Hope Cemetery, 1985

[149] Snyder, ed., *Northumberland County in the American Revolution*

[150] Henry, *March to Quebec*

[151] See Callahan, North, *Daniel Morgan, Ranger of the Revolution*, NY, 1961, and Custis G.W. Parke, *Recollections and Private Memoirs of Washington*, NY, 1860, pp. 261-262

[152] Custis, *Recollections*, pp. 310-319

[153] *Clinton Papers*, Vol. IV, p. 616

[154] Heitman, *Historical Register*, p. 268

[155] *Clinton Papers*, Vol. IV, pp. 223-22

[156] Simms, *History of Schoharie County*, pp. 325

[157] Ward, Christopher, *The War of the Revolution*

[158] Heitman, *Historical Register*, p. 169

[159] Ibid, p. 268

[160] Ibid, p. 368

[161] Ibid, p. 217

[162] Ibid, p. 131

[163] Ibid, p. 68

[164] Ibid, p. 366

[165] Ibid, p. 119

[166] Simms, *Frontiersmen* Vol. II, pp. 412-413

[167] An eyewitness account, Fredericktown, MD.; see Dillin, *The Kentucky Rifle*

[168] Simms, *Frontiersmen*, Vol. II; *History of Schoharie County*, pp. 367

[169] Simms, *Frontiersmen*, Vol. II, p. 392

[170] Ibid, p. 418

[171] Schoharie County church records

[172] Simms, *Frontiersmen*, Vol. II, pp. 633-634

[173] Revolutionary War Pension Files, National Archives, Deposition of William Leek

[174] Ibid, Deposition of Zachariah Tufts

[175] Roscoe, William, *History of Schoharie County*

[176] Sigsby, William, *Life and Adventures of Timothy Murphy, the Benefactor of Schoharie,* 1839, pp. 9-11

[177] Simms, *Frontiersmen*, Vol. II, p. 427

[178] Sigsby, William, *Life and Adventures of Timothy Murphy*, pp. 20-22

[179] Ibid, pp. 24-25

[180] Revolutionary War Pension Files, National Archives, Deposition of Zachariah Tufts; also unpublished research of James Morrison, 1981

[181] Deposition of Joseph Evans, Revolutionary War Pension Files, National Archives

[182] Ibid

[183] Simms, *Frontiersmen*, Vol. II, p. 429

[184] Unpublished research of James Morrison, 1981

[185] O'Brien, Michael J., *Timothy Murphy, Hero of the Revolution*, NY

[186] Sigsby, *Life and Adventures of Timothy Murphy, pp. 10, 20-22, 24-25*

[187] Unpublished manuscript of Allen Burton

[188] Simms, *Frontiersmen*, Vol. II, pp, 695-696

[189] O'Brien, Michael J. *Timothy Murphy, Hero of the Revolution*, NY

[190] Simms, *Frontiersmen*, Vol. II pp, 696-697

[191] Ibid, p. 188

[192] Ibid, pp. 246-248

[193] Unpublished research of James Morrison

[194] Simms, *Frontiersmen*, Vol. II, pp, 422-423

[195] Ibid, pp. 424-425

[196] Unpublished research of James Morrison, 1981

[197] Schoharie County church records

[198] Simms, *Frontiersmen*, Vol. II, p. 131

[199] Revolutionary War Pension Files, National Archives, Deposition of David Ellison; Beekman, Dow, *Schoharie County Heroes*, Cobleskill, 1929, pp. 14-19

[200] O'Brien, Michael J. *Timothy Murphy, Hero of the Revolution*, NY

[201] For these concurring accounts see the British version of Lamb, Sergeant Roger, *Journal of the American War*, Dublin, 1809, p. 178; for Morgan's descriptions, see Higginbotham, Don, *Daniel Morgan, Revolutionary Rifleman*, Chapel Hill, 1961, pp. 170-171; and for the account of Murphy's children see Simms, *Frontiersmen of New York*, Vol. II, pp. 125-126

[202] Old Stone Fort Museum, Schoharie, New York. This photograph was on display when the author visited the museum in 1985

[203] Simms, *Frontiersmen*, Vol. II, p. 183

[204] *Clinton Papers*, Vol. 6, Albany, 1900, p. 265

[205] Simms, *Frontiersmen*, Vol. II, pp. 427-428

[206] Ibid, p. 183

[207] Unpublished research of James Morrison, 1981

[208] Simms, *Frontiersmen*, Vol. II, p. 418

[209] Unpublished research of James Morrison, 1981

[210] Ibid

[211] Simms, *Frontiersmen*, Vol. II, p. 392

[212] Ibid, p. 183

[213] See Hagan, Edward A., *War in Schohary*, Middleburgh, 1980, for details of this action

[214] Much information can be found on the Hager family from a number of sources, primarily Simms, *Frontiersmen of New York*, Vols. I and II, and *Schoharie County and Border Wars*; Roscoe, *History of Schoharie County*; Hagan, *War in Schohary*; Beekman, *Schoharie County Historical Review*, published by the county's historical society, which has printed numerous articles concerning Hager

Suggested Reading

When creating a work of this nature, scores, perhaps hundreds of sources, major and minor, published and unpublished, are referred to repeatedly. Many of them can be found cited in the endnotes. However, for those with a general interest in the riflemen of the Revolutionary era, the following books are suggested.

Boatner, Mark M. XII, *Encyclopedia of the American Revolution,* NY, 1965

Bolton, Charles K. *The Private Soldier Under Washington,* NY, 1902

Callahan, North. *Daniel Morgan, Ranger of the Revolution,* NY, 1961

Clinton, George. *Public Papers of George Clinton, First Governor of New York,* 10 Vols., ed. by Hugh Hastings, Albany, 1899-1914

Coakley, Robert, and Stetson Conn. *The War of the American Revolution, Narrative, Chronology, and Bibliography,* Washington, D.C., 1975

Cook, Frederick. *Journals of the Military Expedition of Major John Sullivan Against the Six Nations of Indians in 1779,* Auburn, 1887 (Reprinted 2000 by Heritage Books, Inc., Bowie, Md.)

Copeland, Peter. *Working Dress in Colonial and Revolutionary America,* Westport, Conn., 1977

Cruikshank, Ernest. *The Story of Butler's Rangers and the Settlement of Niagara,* Welland, Ontario, 1893

Doddridge, Joseph. *Notes on the Settlements and Indian Wars of the Western Parts of Virginia and Pennsylvania*, 1763-1783, Albany, 1824 (Reprinted 1988 by Heritage Books, Inc., Bowie, Md.)

Dillin, Captain John. *The Kentucky Rifle*, Washington, D.C., 1924

Fleming, Thomas, *Liberty, The American Revoltion*, Viking, NY 1997

Graham, James. *The Life of General Daniel Morgan*, NY, 1859

Graymont, Barbara. *The Iroquois in the American Revolution*, Syracuse, 1972

Hagan, Edward. *War in Schohary*, Middleburgh, NY, 1980

Hanger, Colonel George. *Notes to All Sportsmen*, London, 1814

Henry, John Joseph. *Account Of Arnold's Campaign Against Quebec And Of The Hardships And Sufferings Of That Band Of Heroes Who Traversed The Wilderness Of Maine From Cambridge To The St. Lawrence, In The Autumn Of 1775*, Lancaster, 1812, Reprinted Albany, NY, 1877

Higginbotham, Don. *Daniel Morgan, Revolutionary Rifleman*, Chapel Hill

Kaugman, Henry J. *The Pennsylvania Kentucky Rifle*, Harrisburg, 1960

Ketchum, Richard M. *American Heritage History of the Revolution*, NY, 1958

_____. *Saratoga, Turning Point of America's Revolutionary War*, Henry Holt and Co., NY, 1997

Millis, Walter. *Arms and Men*, NY, 1956

Montross, Lynn. *Rag, Tag, and Bobtail, the Story of the Continental Army*, 1775-1783, NY, 1952

Moore, Warren. *Weapons of the American Revolution,* NY, 1967

Neumann, George C. *The History of Weapons of the American Revolution,* NY, 1972

O'Brien, Michael J. *Timothy Murphy, Hero of the Revolution,* NY, 1941

O'Neil, Paul. *The Frontiersmen,* Time-Life Books, Alexandria, Virgina, 1977

Peterson, Harold L. *The Book of the Continental Soldier,* Harrisburg, 1968

Roosevelt, Theodore. *The Winning of the West,* 4 vols, G. P. Putnam's Sons, 1917

Sigsby, William. *Life and Adventures of Timothy Murphy, the Benefactor of Schoharie,* 1839

Simms, Jeptha. *The Frontiersmen of New York,* 2 vols, Albany, 1883

Simms, Jeptha. *Schoharie County and Border Wars,* Albany, 1845

Stone, William L. *Border Wars of the American Revolution,* NY, 1845

Stone, William L. *Life of Joseph Brant,* 2 vols, NY, 1833

Stroh, Oscar. *Thompson's Rifle Battalion,* Harrisburg

Sullivan, A. M., *Tim Murphy, Morgan Rifleman, and Other Ballads,* The Declan X. McMullen Company, Inc., NY, 1947

Swiggett, Howard, *War Out of Niagara: Walter Butler and the Tory Rangers,* NY, 1933

The Sullivan-Clinton Campaign in 1779, Albany, 1929

Thatcher, James. *Military Journal During the American Revolution, from 1775 to 1783,* Boston, 1823

Trevelyan, George Otto. *The American Revolution*, 6 vols, NY, 1909

Ward, Christopher. *War of the Revolution*, 2 vols., NY 1952

Watt, Gavin K. *The Burning of the Valleys*, Dundern Press, Toronto, 1997

Watt, Gavin, and Ernest Cruickshank. *King's Royal Regiment of New York*, Toronto, 1984

Wright, Col. John Womack. *Some Notes on the Continental Army*, Cornwallville, 1975

Suggested Novels

Brick, John, *The Rifleman,* Doubleday, 1953

Brick, John, *King's Rangers,* Doubleday, 1954

Brick, John, *Captives of the Senecas,* Duell, Sloan, and Pearce, 1964

Brick, John, *On the Old Frontier: A Tim Murphy Adventure,* G. P. Putnam's Sons, 1966

Chambers, Robert W. *Little Red Foot,* Doran, 1921

Chambers, Robert W. *The Hidden Children*

Edmonds, Walter D. *Drums Along the Mohawk,* Little, Brown, 1936

Horan, James. *King's Rebel,* Crown, 1953

Index

HOPEWELL, John 191
HORNE, John 87
HOWEARD, Enos 141
HOWE, Gen 73 Gen William
  14 Sgt John 191 Sgt Maj
  John 181
HOWELL, Cpl Vincent 191
HOWRACAN, Patrick 191
HUBBARD, 181 J Niles 177
HUBLEY, Lt Col Adam 54
HUMPHREYS, 181
HUNGERMAN, Nicholas 63
HUSELEN, Edward 190
HUTT, Robert 114 150
INGLE, Tom xiv
JACOBS, Cpl Rowley 191
  William 192
JEHOIAKIM, Capt 63
JENNINGS, Jonathan 76
JERMAIN, Joelle xiv
JERSEYS, Pursuit Across The
  18
JILES, James 192
JOHNSON, 150-151 166 Capt
  39 Col 185 Col John 120
  Sir John 115 121 132 146
KANADASAGE, 59
KATCHER, Philip 177
KELLY, Cpl John 189
KENDIAN, 59
KENT, Sgt Smith 191
KERR, William 189
KILL-DEVIL, (Beverage) 107
KING, Joseph 190
KING'S MOUNTAIN, 180
KISTNER, Ted xiv 8
KOONEY, Christopher 192
KUSHAY, 60
LACROSSE, Hannah xiv
  Leslie xiv 11 Richard x
LAFAYETTE, 18 79 123
  Marquis De 16
LAKE UTSAYANTHA, 108
  158 167
LATTIMORE, Nancy 112
LAVIOLETTE, Gary xiv

LEE, Edward 190 Gen Charles 12 18
LEEK, 112-116 132 149-150 155 159-
  161 173 Maria 37 116 William 37
  68 77 106 111 127 131 142 147
  150 153-154 162 166 185-187 192
LESSON, Dwaine xiv
LEWIS, Gen Andrew 72
LIFE OF BRANT, (book) 158
LIFE-GUARD, Washington's 95-96
LINCOLN, Gen 103 Gen Benjamin
  122
LINN, William 189
LITTLE BEARD'S TOWN, 61 63-66
  (Genesee Castle) 86 92
LIVINGSTON, 185 Gov 45
LLOYD, 115 132 151 Elizabeth 72
  William 106 114 147-150 162 185
LLOYD (LOYD), Pvt William 191
LOCKWOOD, Frank xiv
LONG, 97-98 Capt 20 23 79 96 106
  112 118 123 129 181 188 Capt
  Gabriel 3 36 74 95 102 127 145
  149 152 154 180 188 190 Ens
  Reuben 191 Gabriel 19 Lt 33 Lt
  Reuben 31 99 188 Pvt Reuben
  192 Reuben 101 Sgt Nicholas
  191
LONG ISLAND, Leek At Battle Of
  111 Murphy At Battle Of 135
  Murphy In Battle Of 142
LONG KNIVES, 72
LONGRIFLE, 5-6 vs Musket 6
LOUDON, Capt John 76
LOWDON, 78 Capt John 111 142
LOWER FORT, 26 120 151
LYON, John 192 Lt 78
M'KONDY, John 87
MACDONALD, 165
MACHIN, Capt Thomas 39
MADISON, President 76
MATTICE, Miss 37 147
MCCAW, Patrick 189
MCCLANAHAN'S REGIMENT, 122

Made in the USA
Charleston, SC
27 January 2013